Sweet Little Girl

Celine Miller

Copyright © 2024 by Celine Miller

All rights reserved.

No portion of this book may be reproduced in any form without written permission from the publisher or author, except as permitted by U.S. copyright law.

Contents

One	1
Two	6
Three	9
Four	12
Five	17
Six	21
Seven	25
Eight	29
Nine	34
Ten	39
Eleven	42
Twelve	46
Thirteen	50
Fourteen	55
Fifteen	59

Sixteen	65
Seventeen	69
Eighteen	74
Nineteen	78
Twenty	82
Twenty one	86
Twenty Two	91
Twenty Three	95
Twenty Four	100
Twenty Five	104
Twenty Six	111
Twenty Seven	115
Twenty Eight	119
Twenty Nine	123
Thirty	128
Thirty One	133

One

"Ouch! I swore I switched off the stove."

Living alone was the best decision I've ever made for myself. Well... besides the days where I had to remember to do things around the house, like switching off the stove. I loved living with my grandmother, the only downside was the fact that my dad lived under the same roof. That's a whole story for another day.

About me? Well I love food but hate making it so I end up eating and spending a lot of money on junk food. I can't really cook so junk works just fine for me, I'm my own boss. I have only 1 because I'm not too good with relationships. I'm soo glad that she still sticks around because I'm basically a nucklehead.

Hafsa, my best friend and only friend, had invited me to her birthday dinner. To say I'm anxious is an understatement. I'm usually fine around people of my age group not so much with older people. I'm used to being around Hafsa's mom so I'm fairly comfortable around her. The issue tonight is going to be meeting the rest of her family.

"Hafsa I don't think I'll be able to make it" I say fake coughing, hoping she'll fall for my tricks.

"Nollani! You'll need to do better if you want me to believe those lies sweetie." Hafsa says with a bored tone.

"Hafsa please... I'm too scared. I'll make it up to you, I'll take you out to your favourite restaurant and we can have the most fun ever and we can eat all the food in the w-"

"-NOLLANI! We! Are not doing that today" Hafsa says practically scolding me. How dare she.

"Why are you being mean to me?!" I whine through the phone throwing myself on the bed.

"Dramatic as always." She says and I can literally see her rolling her eyes through this phone. "You better be ready by 7 pm I'll be there 10 minutes before 7. Dinner starts at 8 pm, Lani I'm warning you if you're not ready..."

"But Hafsa..."

"No! Be ready or I'll tell my mother you're being a brat."

"Okay, you don't have to tell her all that. Why are you so bossy."

"Bye Lani." She screams in excitement and disconnected the call before I could respond. What a little bi-

buzz

I hear the dryer buzzing telling me it's done. Great now I have to fold the laundry. I'll just put them on the bed, I'll do that tomorrow. I swear. The day goes by with me just scrolling through social media. I get up to start getting ready 20 minutes before Hafsa arrives, not the best decision...

I pick out my new pastel pink dress and a matching ribbon for my hair. I'm not too sure what shoes I want to wear but I pick out Mary Janes and white ruffled socks. I pack my backpack because I'll be sleeping over at Hafsa's tonight. It won't be like our regular sleepover because there will be a few of her family members staying over.

After a quick shower, I lather my body with lotion and start getting dressed. Once I'm done, I try tying my hair into a high bun but it's just not sleeking down. I sigh in frustration, my arms are hurting. I look at the clock and it looks like Hafsa's a minute late.

"Now why are you still doing your hair!" I jump startled. Did I forget to lock the door?

"My hair isn't cooperating" I say looking at her and wailing in frustration.

"Here let me help" She starts working the brush and gel through my hair and before I even know it she done. My hair wasn't doing that for me, it's not even sticky from the gel. What in the witch-craftsmanship did she do to my hair. She puts my little gold earrings on for me. She pats my shoulders signalling she's done.

"Let's g- aww look how adorable you are" she says in an annoying babyish voice.

"Shut up! Why aren't you dressed? And why do you still have rollers in your hair?" I look at her puzzled.

"Well if you keep interrogating me I'll look like this for the rest of the night, LETS GO!" I drag myself behind her. She's so annoying!

When we get to Hafsa's House, there's a lot going on but the biggest takeaway is that it looks so beautiful. I wish my family cared this much about my birthday. I leave Hafsa to go get ready while I go to her mom to say hi and possibly help where I can.

"Hi Aunty Jasmine!" I shout excited to see her, I saw her like 2 days ago but who cares. She turns full force slightly alarmed by my sudden noise.

"Nollani!" She looks at me sternly before she embraces me in a warm fluffy hug. Well fluffy because, I mean... ugh whatever. "How are you my love? You look so adorable" she says cooing at me.

"Aunty Jasmine stooop! I say feeling the warmth on my cheeks. She only chuckles. "Can I help you pleeease?" I ask with my hands intwined.

"Sure only if you promise to be carefull little miss clumsy" I hate when she calls me that but I don't do it intentionally. I responded with a quick nod before going in and helping her with the food. There were people working around the house, some decorating, others helping with setting the table and a few placing the ready made food on the table.

With everything almost done, guests start coming in bit by bit and eventually the house is buzzing with chatter and laughter. Before I get overwhelmed I leave to go find Hafsa. I walked into her room and oh my days was she beautiful. She was draped in a tight fitting sparkly dusty pink dress that went all the way down just above her ankles.

"You look so beautiful Hafsa!" I say holding back tears. I felt like a mom seeing their baby's first steps.

"Thank you my sweetie, now stop staring and let's go." I leave ahead of her so the spotlight is only on her and not the pair of us. As soon as she walked out everyone was in awe. She really deserves all this attention she's just so pure and so humble.

After she greets her family we move on to take our places at the table. I obviously sat next to Hafsa but the seat next to me was empty. That slightly made my heart sore because no one wants to sit next to me. Oh well whatever.

A few minutes later Hafsa jumps off her chair screaming "Aunty Naina" before she hugs the Naina lady. Aunty Jasmine gets up from her chair giving the unknown lady a hug. She's very beautiful I must say.

"Well you're very early Hanaina!" Aunty Jasmine says sarcastically making the lady laugh. I wonder if she's Aunty Jasmine's sister? Maybe her cousin? I shrug my shoulders going back to my plate of food.

Two

A few seconds later I'm stuck in between Hafsa and her 'Aunty Hanaina'. There was a lot going on at the dinner table. Hafsa was having a conversation about who knows what, so I was just having my food not wanting any attention on me anyway. Jokes on me though because seconds later I'm asked what my name is.

"Nollani" I say not looking up still not wanting any attention on me.

"Oh Nollani! Sounds familiar." The woman next to me says. "Hafsa do you plan on introducing me?" Hanaina says sounding disappointed.

"Aunty Naina, I'm sorry" my best friend responds sounding innocent. "Lani this is my Aunty Naina she's my mom's very close friend. Aunty Naina I'm sure you know Lani now so no need for me to introduce her to you." Hanaina nods leaving Hafsa to continue with her previous conversation.

"Why are you being so shy with me? Am I making you uncomfortable?" Yes you are, "If so I can leave you alone." She says ever so softly. I turn to respond but I freeze when I'm met with the most beautiful dark eyes and perfect sweet smile. All that was going through my head now was how safe this woman felt. As much as I didn't want to talk to anyone, I don't mind her.

I took in her whole appearance. She was dressed in a long sleeved off the shoulder white maxi dress that showed her perfect shape. Her hair was long and dark which matched her eyes. She wore glasses which probably was the reason she looked so stern but her words were sweet. She's pretty tall compared to me who's just sitting at 143 cm.

I quickly realise that I'm ogling her and look away quickly apologising. The response I get is a "You're fine bubba" which makes me want to melt. She smiles before carrying on with her own conversation with Aunty Jasmine.

I can't help but stress over the fact that she may think I don't feel comfortable with her. I want to tell her she doesn't make me uncomfortable at all but I'm too scared to speak to her. She probably thinks I'm very weird too! Why did I just stare at her like that? I'm so dumb!

I'm listening to her speak, even though she wasn't speaking to me. She has a very soothing voice I can't help but feel jealous that she isn't paying attention to me anymore. I have no idea why I feel like that but I do. Hafsa checks on me to see if I'm still doing okay which I assure her I'm fine.

The night goes by with a few toasts and speeches which I'm so glad Hafsa didn't put me in the spotlight for. That's until she was thanking everyone for coming and roughly pulled me boldly telling everyone I was her bestfriend and a whole lot of cheesy nonsense. I was just standing there looking awkward. She finally lets go of me, thanks to her dad who sends her upstairs to get something.

Hafsa's dad wasn't around a lot because he's always out on business. Unlike the relationship I have with his wife, my relationship with him is cordial. I really envy his relationship with his daughter. Knowing him has shown me that not all men are airheads.

It was pretty late so it was just a few of us sitting around. Hafsa told me a bit about Hanaina. Turns out she lives around here and is an entrepreneur, sis has her own money. I wonder why I've never seen her here before. Hafsa did speak about an aunt of hers, she just didn't say who.

I head to the bathroom hoping to get some time alone. I stay in the bathroom for a pretty long time before Hafsa comes looking for me. "Lani? Are you okay?" She asks storming in joining me in the empty bathtub.

"Yeah I'm fine, it's just been a very long night" I softy whine resting my head on Hafsa's shoulder with my eyes closed.

"Maybe you should get to bed it is pretty late now."

"No! I'm not sleepy! Mean!" I respond before realising seconds later, that wasn't Hafsa speaking. I shoot up and look at the door way, it's Hanaina. I did say this woman makes me feel some type of way...

"Oh I'm so mean aren't I?" She walks in amused by my reaction. I look away shyly listening to Hafsa giggling at my slip of words.

"Hafsa your mother is looking for you love, I'll just stay here and talk to miss meanie." Hanaina says teasingly. Before I could even protest Hafsa leaves. There she goes throwing me under the bus.

Three

All I wanted to happen right now was for the ground to swallow me. " I just wanted to apologise for making you think you made me feel uncomfortable at the table, that wasn't the case at all. I just thought you looked beautiful and you were one of the very few people that were so kind to me." I quickly say all in one breath, I probably said too much, ugh! I'm swiftly picked up and sat on the basin counter.

"What the hell" I say squealing.

"You're okay pumpkin." If she keeps calling me these names I'm going to feel small and then she's gonna think I'm a weirdo all over again. "I'm glad you told me that because I wanted to apologise for making you feel uncomfortable, you beat me to it." She smiled fixing her glasses.

She had this strong mommy like aura. I've never had a mommy before and surely never met one, but she makes me wanna lay on her chest and just snuggle into her. "I'm up here Nollani" She says with a smirk.

"Sow- sorry" I say looking at my hands on my lap. She swiftly takes me off the counter again and sets me on my feet. This lady and her strength!

"If we're done with this very short conversation, let's go you need to get to bed." she lets me lead the way and I do so proudly. I go over to a snoring Hafsa who's sprawled on the couch with drool running down her face. This girl. I shake her awake leading us upstairs. The older women are left gossiping downstairs while Hafsa and I head to bed.

The next time I open my eyes the room is extremely bright. I question my where abouts before my brain answers all it's questions. I'm reminded about everything that happened last night. Atleast everyone is gone and I don't have to hide from anyone.

"Wake up old hag, gosh I thought you loved food, why are you not at the breakfast table?" I shoot up looking at my stupid alarm clock of a friend.

"Food? I haven't had some of that in a while." I say jumping off the bed to take a quick morning shower - which this dummy appears to have taken already - before I go get some of Aunty Jasmine's delicious cooking.

"Good morning your majesty!" Aunty Jasmine says before I sit down for some food. My my did I not stuff my face. The food was so good.

"Mumma did you know Lani doesn't make any food..." I try to cover her mouth but she holds my head way at arms length and I just can't reach her. "-she doesn't make food for herself and buys lots of junk that ruins her appetite so she stays 'full'." Wow my own friend.

"That's very naughty of her" I hear someone say. I turn to look and I'm met with stern dark disapproving eyes. I look away feeling my cheeks flush and being called naughty by Hanaina.

"Nollani!" Aunty Jasmine says sounding dissapointed. "That's why I asked you to come live with us, you don't take care of yourself." The way I feel like wringing Hafsa's neck. I turn to her and mouth bitch. Which causes her to giggle.

I really appreciated Aunty Jas and Uncle Tim's offer but I didn't want to burden them. They've already been so kind to me many times I just don't want to make them feel like they're over extending themselves.

I'm pretty much a burden already but they just don't say. My dad doesn't even call to check if I'm alive, he has never been present for me. I've always relied on myself so being independent comes easily for me. I understand how irresponsible I can be sometimes but that's how it's going to stay. My mother passed away so he's the only parent I have. In my head I'm an orphan. I guess that's how it was supposed to be for me.

"Nollani? What do you think?" Hanaina asks. I look around confused but answer before things get awkward and embarrassing for me.

"Yes that's right" I say not even sure what I'm consenting to. I look around the room and everyone is shocked. "What?" I whispered to Hafsa who is just as shocked. Embarrassed myself anyway I guess.

Four

Hanaina's Pov

"I think since I live alone she can stay with me and I can monitor her and her eating habits. Nollani? What do you think?" I ask hoping she agrees.

Jasmine told me a bit about Nolani. The reason why her and I have never really met is because of her background. Yasmina only wanted to create a safe space for her thus she didn't invited me while she was visiting. She didn't want to invited someone else while she was round and make her feel uncomfortable.

She didn't go into much detail because she thought it wasn't her place to talk about Nollani's family history, which was a decision I understood and respected. Nollani is a very sweet girl, it only hurts me that she's had people hurt her in the past. The poor baby.

I loved interacting with her, she was shy which I found adorable but I also caught the fact that she slipped slightly when I met her and Hafsa in the bathroom last night. If I connect the dots I could probably reach the conclusion that she's a little but that would be a drastic assumption.

I know my request to get her to come live with me was sudden but it was only a joke. I know she wasn't paying attention and just answered to not show that she had completely lost the conversation along the way.

"You're willing to live with someone you hardly spent time with but didn't want to take my offer?" Jasmine said evidently upset. Nollani looked just as confused before realisation hit her.

"Mumma this bimbo wasn't paying attention and just answered anyhow, you know what she's like sometimes." Hafsa says defending her friend. I know I had asked jokingly but deep down I wanted to keep this little pumpkin where I could see her. I understand her situation, so I need to keep my mommy feelings and reflexes tucked away.

I leave an hour later just to go check if my office is running smoothly. I'm wearing a white collared shirt with a nude pleated skirt and few gold accessories. I get to the office and immediately everyone starts buzzing around going to their designated places. I look around very unpleased before going up to my office. My assistant walks in a few seconds later.

"Morning Miss Zalda wh- " I cut her off just there.

"Why was everyone sitting around not working early in the morning when I had given strict orders to make sure everything is under control while I'm not here. I'm only an hour and a few minutes late Latisha!" I scold her. If I could I would've already warmed her bum.

"I'm sorry Miss Zalda I -"

"You what? Stop trying to make excuses for failing to carry out a simple task young lady! This better be the last time this happens while I'm not around or there will be trouble. Am I understand Latisha Amanda Rein?"

"Yes Miss Zalda, I'll make sure nothing of this nature ever happens again" She says with her cheeks looking slightly flushed.

"Very well." I respond with a nod. Please close my door behind you Latisha." I ask having calmed down slightly. I know I can be a pain in the backside sometimes but I like when everything goes right. I want no nonsense. I don't like feeling like I'm running a preschool when I'm running a serious business. I have to be strict sometimes.

I manage 3 meetings, 2 of which were scheduled to take place and 1 that I agreed to squeeze in today. I decide I've heard enough talking for one day so I head to my office to get some paperwork done. I decide to get my phone to check a few of my messages. Where on earth did I put it? I ring Latisha to come into my office, walking in a second later.

"Have you seen my phone? Or where I happened to have placed it when I came?" I ask her while scanning my desk for it.

"No I haven't, but I can go check in your car?"

"Yes! I must have left it in the car." I say digging for my car keys and handing them to her. I continued with my work before Latisha comes in empty handed. "I looked everywhere. It's not there."

"Huh. That's weird." Where on eart- oh Jasmine's. Great now I have to leave the office again. It was already pretty late in the afternoon so it wouldn't hurt to leave for a few minutes. "I'll be back in a few minutes Tisha, you better make sure there's no horseplay while I'm gone." I sternly state. Her response is a very quick nod with a nervous grin. Goodness this girl, she's responsible for the most part but she can get a bit silly sometimes.

I finally grab my bag and leave, driving to Jasmine's place. Having to drive in afternoon traffic was a headache, but I get there with my head thankfully still intact. I ring the bell. I wonder if Jas is home, she also works pretty late some days.

"Aunty Hanaina? What's wrong?" Hafsa says peeking out the door. I frown before I push her aside. What is this child up to?

"Hafsa?! I stare at her in shock. "Why on earth is the house flooded?" I spot Nollani somewhere in the back trying to clean up the water looking anxious and exhausted. I look back at Hafsa who is just as anxious. I sternly tell her to go get towels to clean the mess up. I assume Jas isn't home yet because the house would've been on fire had she seen this mess.

Nollani spots me a second later and panics looking away from me quickly. What the heck were these two up to. "Nollani? What happened here?" I ask her instead because I trust her to be truthful and give me the response I need to hear. She's quiet for a few seconds playing with her fingers.

"It was nothing serious Aunty Naina we were just-" I cut Hafsa off.

"NOLLANI! What happened?" I say evidently unhappy with the two girls, shutting off the lies Hafsa was cooking up.

"I-I was, I thou- thought-"

"She was just-"

"HAFSA! let her speak before you get yourself in much more trouble." I say trying my best to stay calm. Hafsa had mischievous tendencies sometimes so I know she can cook up a good lie. I hate lies so if she even tries to fool me it won't end well.

"I I I thought the washing machine was done but it it still had water when I opened it." Oh my goodness this child.

"Nollani." I say unsure of how I want to address her silly little mistakes. She guiltily looked away fiddling with the towel in her hands. "Alright then. You both better clean this mess before your mother comes back." I say looking in Hafsa's direction. I manage to help where I can, and thankfully after sometime all the water's gone.

I shaking my head slightly, looking at them. Hafsa giggles. While Nollani goes to put everthing back in it's place. Jas walks in a second later she looks at the three of us confused.

"Naina? Why are you here? The house looks and smells clean. Aww girls!" she looks at Hafsa and Nollani who look sheepishly at me. Probably afraid I would tell jasmine about the little accident.

"I couldn't find my phone so I came to check if I left it here this morning."

"Ohhh I know where it is Aunty Naina, I'll go get it." Hafsa rushes out the room.

"Well you might as well stay for dinner before leaving it is a few minutes past 7pm."

"Jas I have some work left to do. My assistant is probably waiting for me. Probably even wondering why I'm not back yet." I tell her not sure if she's fully convinced. Hafsa hands me my phone. So sweet of her because it's fully charged.

"Naina, it's late already you can't be working this late you'll burn out. Come join us for dinner I ordered sea food. " I let out a sigh of defeat.

"Fine let me call my assistant." I leave for a bit to call Latish and come back once everything is sorted. The girls set up the table. I plate up the food while Yasmina changes into house clothes.

I sit opposite Nollani this time around. I wanted to help her with her food but I respect boundaries so I let her eat watching her making a little mess on her shirt. Pretty cute to me. I leave shortly after, wanting nothing but my bed. I get home, taking a quick hot shower. I jump into bed and sleep like a baby.

Five

"Shoot I'll be late."

Well quick update, Hafsa and I had volunteered to help Naina at her office since we had recess for a month. We didn't get to sit in an office like everyone else. We had a table that we both shared which was set directly opposite 'Miss Hanaina's' office. She usually left her door open so she could keep an eye on us.

We usually got to the office right before Hanaina which was the instruction she had given us during our orientation. Hafsa bailed out since she had decided to take an online course on digital marketing. This is the first day without her and I'm already running late. Just great.

I arrive at the office and everyone is already working, I head to our work area. Thankfully her door is closed, I think to myself going to sit down.

"Nollani! Come in here please." How the heck did she know. Did I tell you how scary Hanaina is in the office. I could just evaporate. I walk in and close the door behind me.

"Why are we late?" she asks not looking up. I stay silent thinking of an excuse. She pushes her chair backwards and turns facing to her right crossing her legs so elegantly. "Come here please." She says very calm. I walk around her desk and stand in front of her.

She stares above her glasses, right into my soul. "Usually when I ask questions I expect an answer. Am I supposed to get it out of you myself or are you going to speak?" She asks calmly. What does she mean get it out of me herself? Crazy woman.

"I was... um ... stuck in traffic?" I say unsure of what to say. I'm such an idiot is that the best I could do. Ugh!

"No." She shakes her head slightly, "try again." She says looking angry. This lady is such a mommy. I wonder if she knows what a-. "NOLLANI!" She yells uncrossing her legs.

"IwaslatebecauseIsleptlateandcouldn'twakeupthismorning!" I quickly say all in one breath. She looks at me with a raised eyebrow.

"Why did you sleep late?" She asks very calm which scares me.

"I was watching Netflix." I say looking away. Stupid Tinkerbell series.

"What time did you sleep?" Why does she even care.

"Pretty late-"

"What time did you sleep?" I gulp hearing her repeat her question.

"I don't remember but the last time I remember seeing was 3 am and some minutes." I say shrugging my shoulders. She says something under her breath, I couldn't really hear it so I'm not bothered.

"We are gonna work on that, I want you to take your chair and place it right next to me. From now on you're going to be working in my office." Oh fuck me! Right next to her? I stand frozen in front of her. "Now young lady!" She says in an scary mommy voice. So mean I pout mentally.

I quickly get the chair and place it next to her. I nervously sit next to her. I turn my head in her direction and I'm met with her boobies. They're big. She clears her throat making me realise I was staring at... them. I feel my cheeks tingling.

"I just need you to do some excel work. I'll give you one of my laptops. You'll be using it until you finish." She shows me what to do. It's pretty easy, but it's difficult to concentrate sitting next to her. "Are you going to manage. I nod. "Use your words dear. I can't hear nodding now can I?"

"No, I'm sorry Miss Hanaina." I say feeling slightly small.

"You're alright pumpkin." She says making me blush, I whine mentally. Why is she calling me these sweet names.

"Oh you're such a big girl aren't you? don't need to be called sweet names!" She says teasingly. I freeze realising I spoke out loud. Her teasing just makes me feel even little. She has a smirk seeing my frustration. It's not funny I'm really trying to work, why is she distracting me with her teasing.

I start working with the little focus I have left. It's a little nerve wrecking working next to her. I shake my head a bit trying to stay big but it's just too hard while she's next to me. I play with my pen a few times before I realise I'm distracted and go back to work.

This is hard to do this without Hafsa. I try my hardest to work but it's just making my brain tired. Miss Hanaina gets up grabbing a few documents from her cupboard and sits on her chair again. I look at her fantasising about sitting on her lap which isn't helping my situation.

"Why aren't you working she says with her eyes glued to her laptop. I quickly look at the laptop in front of me seeing the little work I've done. I look up at her and see her looking at the very same thing. I've already gotten in trouble today.

She looks back at me sternly with her eyebrow raised. I shrink under her gaze my head feeling very fuzzy. I can't be small right now! I shake my head trying to focus but I'm too far gone.

"What's wrong?" She asks acting like she didn't just make me slip. Her full attention is now on me.

"I no no" I say shrugging. I feel tears burning my eyes once I realise what I just said. Well now she probably thinks I'm more weird I couldn't even hold back my tears anymore.

"Hey, you're okay sweet girl." She says pulling me into her for a hug. I'm taken by surprise but hide my face into her chest letting her rub my back. Her steady heartbeat ever so soothing. I wish I could get this everyday. "You're fine bubba, you're fine."

Six

I get to work on time this morning. Everthing that happened yesterday was embarrassing. I can't believe I slipped and cried in front of her. She drove me home and gave me strict instructions to sleep at 9pm sharp. I listened because I knew she was going to get me to tell the truth somehow had I not listened to her.

I listen to music as I get ready. I hop out of the shower and get ready in a little yellow dress and a white cardigan with matching frilly white socks and pumps. I tie my hair in a high bun before packing my bag.

I leave requesting an uber to the local coffee shop that's located a few minutes away from the office. I get a coffee with a slice of chocolate cake. Not the best breakfast but I like it so I'm gonna have it. I walk to the office finishing my coffee and cake.

I promise myself not to accidentally regress today. I can't embarrass myself twice consecutively. I sit in my chair right next to hers and start working.

At 9 am sharp she walks in. She looks beautiful. She's dressed in a tight black skirt suit with matching black stiletto heels. Her hair is parted in the middle and curled dramatically. Her first two buttons are undone of course I'd notice that. She's so perfect.

"Staring is rude." She says taking off her blazer, hanging it on her chair. She smells so good I say in my head not caring that I'm still staring. "Nollani?" I look up at her.

"Yes mom- ma'am." What the hell, I almost called her mommy.

"I'm proud of you for getting to work on time. Good girl." She smiles.

"Thank you." I smile shyly.

The day goes on with us doing our own work. She leaves and comes back with a cup of coffee for herself and two sandwiches for the both of us. We sit on her office couch and eat in comfortable silence. I have a sip of my water and continue with my work. She comes around sitting on her chair and finishes off her coffee.

Latisha comes in to discuss something with her. I don't really pay much attention to it because I'm distracted by my own silly thoughts. I've gotten to know Tisha these past few days, while Hafsa was around. She's really fun and lets me hang out with them. Well Lydia is way more fun but I still like Tisha more.

Lydia's one of Tisha's friends. She has a huge crush on Naina it's so funny. She always asks Tisha about Naina, and says weird things like letting Hanaina step on her. Naina doesn't really like me sitting with them saying they're way older than me but I do anyway, she's not my boss! Well she sorta is but still!

I reach for my bag that's placed at my feet, trying to get a notebook to write down a few of the tasks I need to complete tonight when I get home. Something goes very wrong. How I ended up on the floor was a mystery to me. Hanaina looks at me just as surprised. I look back at her sheepishly, embarrassed to say the least. I get up quickly sitting on my chair again, the notebook completely forgotten about.

"Are you okay? What were you doing?" She asks putting her glasses on her head. I respond with a shrug. The way I keep embarrassing myself in front of her, ugh! Aunty Yas was so right about me being clumsy. "Does it hurt anywhere?" She asks. My knees hurt because I landed on them but I'm not telling her that.

"No." I say shaking my head. She shakes her head and continues with her work.

I do a lot of my work, catching up on what I couldn't do yesterday. I look over at Hanaina and she's still super busy. I'm so bored, maybe I can check my social media just to pass some time. I grab my bag - carefully this time - putting it on my lap using my phone.

"You better not make me angry Nollani!" I jump startled closing my bag and quickly place it by my feet. I huff because I only managed to unlock my phone. Fuck her and her office. She's paying me though so... not really 'fuck her'.

I push myself to work a little bit more before completely losing motivation. I fold my arms and look up at the scary lady next to me I don't know what I wanted her to do but I wanted her to pay attention to me.

"Young lady why are you not working?" She asks looking down at me. I respond with a shrug. "Words." She says in her mommy voice making my insides tingle.

"Too tired! No want to work anymore!" I say throwing my hands in the air. "Me wanna colour, this boring" I pout at her unhappy that I have to tell her everything.

"Oh is that so?" She ask. I respond with a nod crossing my arms again. "With that attitude maybe you need to go stand in the corner where cheeky little girls belong." She says scooping me onto her lap. I shrug not moved by her threat. I lean onto her feeling warmth in my chest. Maybe this was the attention I wanted.

"Me too big! I not go in the corner". I say playing with her undone buttons. I can slightly see her cleavage but she lets me play with her buttons so I continue.

"No. You are not too big for corner time" She says smirking at me. "but... if that's the case then maybe I should give you a spanking instead. A lesson to not act sassy with me" She says with a lifted eyebrow. The image in my head of me her spanking me scares me. I don't like the idea one bit. I lean into her hiding my face.

"No, thank you!" I say quickly shaking my head.

She chuckles softly. "I thought so." She says patting my bottom. I sit in her lap for the quite a long time. I felt a bit drowsy but fight my sleep.

"Come pumpkin, let's get you something fun to do. Yes?" I nod quickly, letting her set me down. I really want her to be my mommy but don't think she's knows I'm a little, so this is as far as we're gonna get.

Seven

Hanaina's POV

I've enjoyed having Nollani around me. One thing I now know for sure is that she's a little and goodness did she love Tinkerbell. As much as I appreciate her working for me, I don't think I can let her continue. Reason being the fact that she regresses a lot which means she doesn't really finish her work. She's regressed multiple times throughout this week. I know that she regresses involuntary, which tells me that she feels safe and comfortable around me.

I'm going to take a big decision today. I don't know how to tell her I don't want her working for me anymore. It worries me a lot that she lives alone and won't budge to Jasmine's offer. She doesn't eat right and has to uber to work and back home everyday which I find to be unsafe.

I've been getting her lunch during break otherwise she'll just eat junk. I also have been taking her home after work since the beginning of this week, it's the safest option and I don't want anything to happen to her. I've decided to invite Nollani to my place today since it's Saturday, just to let her know she won't be working for me anymore.

I feel guilty but I know this has to be done. I go into my office to get some work done. I told Nollani to come over to help me with some paperwork just for today but the poor girl doesn't know I'm about to let her go. I'm anxiously waiting for her to arrive while I finish off my work.

I manage to discuss some issues with my current supplier before moving on to discuss different issues with my second supplier. I look at the clock before I decide to prepare some lunch for when Nollani comes by. I decide to prepare chicken wraps with a chilli sauce. I don't really know if she likes spicy food but I'll see when she gets here. I pop some potato chips in the oven to cook. I decide to make brownies because why not.

I decide to take another shower while the brownies get ready in the oven. I hop out the shower going downstairs to check my brownies aren't burning. They look fine so I go back to get dressed. I decide to wear a black button down shirt which I tucked into my black flowy pants and pointed heels. I get the brownies out the oven before I go back to doing my make up and hair.

I part my hair in the middle and tie it into a bun at the back. I put my glasses on and head downstairs to watch something before little miss arrives. I don't wait too long before I hear my door bell. I open the door to see Nollani dressed in a cute short pastel pink strappy dress with a short sleeved white top underneath.

"Hi" She says so sweet.

She looks so adorable I could just eat her up. She hands me a bouquet of fresh flowers that she hid behind her back. I smile thanking her. I see her playing with the hem of her dress so I try to loosen her up.

"Did you have something to eat dear? I'm a bit starved. Would you like to join me for lunch?" I ask her. She nods her head. "Sorry couldn't hear that." I say with a raised eyebrow. She shrinks back.

"Yes Miss Hanaina." She says not looking at me.

"Alright, come here baby" I lead her to my dinning table. Pulling out a chair for her to sit. I serve her food placing the hot sauce in front of us. I pour some juice for her while I get myself wine.

I sit down right next to her immediately sensing her nervousness. Why is she so nervous? she's used to being around me, maybe in a different setting but nonetheless.

She takes a bite of her wrap, juices run down her chin. I quickly grab a napkin wiping the sauce off her chin. She dips it into the hot sauce. "Hot! It's hot baby!" I say she takes a bite and smiles at me but quickly gulps her juice after. I chuckle at her silliness before continuing with my food. I need her to stay big so I don't have to postpone this conversation.

I wait for her to finish, she eats pretty slow so I take my plate and hers to the kitchen, once she's done. I'll wash them a little later. I give her a brownie and see her eyes sparkle. She says thank you before finishing it in one second. "Nollani." I say surprised. She hides her face. She has crumbs all over her dress. I dust her off shaking my head holding back a laugh.

"Sweetheart can I talk to you?"

"Yes Miss Hanaina" She responds sweetly. We move to the couch.

"Nollani, I know I said I wanted you to help with some paperwork but I don't need you to help me with anything. I wanted to talk to you about something." She looks at me confused. " don't want you to get upset sweetheart but I don't think working at the office is the best thing for you." I see her slump her shoulder, she doesn't respond but looks down at her hands.

"I'm weird aren't I, I can't even do my work right?" She says her eyes welling up with tears.

"No sweetheart that's not the case at all." I quickly say. "I really appreciate how hard you worked my love but, if you continue to regress then you really can't get anything done." She continues playing with her fingers. "Are you familiar with the term little?" I look at her. Her cheeks turn red which answers my question. She nods confirming my assumption.

"Are you a little?" I ask already knowing her answer. She nods again still not giving me any eye contact. "Nollani can you talk to me dear, I want to know what's on your mind right now."

"I don't know." She responds softly. I nod at her response looking down at my own hands.

"Would you let me be your mommy?" I ask, earning all her attention this time.

Eight

What? One minute I'm getting fired the next she's asking me if I would let her be my mommy? The obvious part to all of this is I've wanted to her to be my mommy but this is a lot for one day.

If I agree to her being my mommy, does that mean I lose all my independence? Can I really trust Hanaina? She's been so nice to me though so I don't see why I wouldn't trust her. I have so many questions for her. My hands feel so sweaty. I don't know what's going on in my head.

"I'm sorry baby for rushing you into things. I shouldn't have said that." I stay quiet wiping my hands on my dress. Why can't I just tell her I want her to be my mommy. I've never really had anyone care for me like that. I've supported myself for the most part how do I switch from that?

"Why don't I drive you home?" She says quickly standing up, leaving to probably get her keys.

"No!" I say using my small bit of courage. My stomach feels so funny. I think I'm going to throw up.

"No?" She asks confused turning on her heels.

"No!" I repeat myself.

She looks at me intensely waiting for me to continue. "I- I- want you to be my-" Why is it so difficult to say. I'm so stupid! Maybe she should really drive me home.

"I need you to tell me what you want lovebug" She comes over to me rubbing my back. I just want to jump in her lap and have her hold me like she did a few days ago.

"-my mommy, Iwantyoutobemymommy." I say not making eye contact with her. My face feels wet, why am I crying? She pulls me onto her lap and cradles me.

"You're overwhelmed huh?" She softly asks patting my bottom. "I would gladly be your mommy baby, I just need to hear what's going on in your head." She kisses my head making me feel so little.

"My head too noisy" I say sitting up and facing her, rubbing the top of my head.

"Is that so? What's all the noise about, can you tell me?" She turns me so that I'm straddling her lap. I lay my head on her chest trying very hard to focus but I can't.

"No hurts." I say whining rubbing my face on her chest.

"It's alright pumpkin" she says bouncing me on her lap which makes me very sleepy. She continues bouncing me and patting my bottom simultaneously. My eyes feel so heavy, then everything feels so quiet.

It's so soft, I open my eyes and I'm surrounded by pillow. Everything looks unfamiliar, where on earth am I?

"Oh shit!"

I slipped. Again! I'll worry about that later. I get off the bed, wondering why it's so high. Stupid bed. I open the door and look down the passage seeing so many doors, some open some closed.

"Nollani?" I hear Hanaina call me. Where is she? I open the door closest to where I hear her voice but she's not there. "Here love!" she yells. I open the next door and I see her sitting at a desk. Of course she has an office in her house! A serious workaholic I must say.

"Did you have a good nap?" She asks looking at me above her glasses.

"Yes Miss Hanaina." Or mommy? I'll ask about that later.

"Can you come over here please, you don't have to stand at the door." She smiles. I stand next to her only to be sat on her lap. I hide my face with my hands. It's different when I'm big, sort of embarrassing.

She chuckles removing my hands from my face. "You have to get used to this if you're going to be my little girl." She smiles at me brushing the hairs out of my face. "I tried to ask when you were little but it wasn't such a great idea, can you tell me what you thought about our conversation earlier?"

"I've never had a mommy before so I don't know how this whole thing works." She nods.

"Well, what happens is you and I consent to this relationship which then means we both agree on a set of rules and boundaries. You can choose if you want to stay independent or you want me to take full control of you and your wants and needs. If you wish to, you can choose to leave this relationship whenever you want. You're not forced to stay pumpkin." I like when she calls me pumpkin. Okay Focus!

"What happens if I choose not to be independent?" I look at her curious.

"Well in that case you can move in with me and let me take care of all your necessities."

"What rules and boundaries are you talking about?" She looks at me for a moment.

"When littles and their caregivers come into agreement, they usually discuss a set of rules and boundaries to avoid anything bad from happening. I'll talk about rules and boundaries with you in great detail a little later." I nod in acknowledgment.

"Have you had a little before?" She freezes before nodding her head.

"Yes, I've had a little one before. She chose to have her big life again so I let her go". I nod not wanting to ask any more questions about her little because it makes me jealous.

"If I move in with you, what's going to happen to my place?" I change the topic.

"We'll let someone else live there then if you ever want to leave I can find you a better place to stay. Then I'll give you all of the savings I have for you so you can support yourself."

"What savings?"

"While you live with me, I'll be supporting you like how any parent would or atleast should. For me, that includes saving money to help fulfil your needs should anything happen in the future." I don't want her money though. I don't think I deserve any of it anyway. I just really like how she makes me feel.

"But I don't want you spending money on me." I tell her with my arms crossed.

"But I will be spending money on you." I shake my head not pleased with her answer. She nods her head, sternly staring at me as if challenging me.

"Fine!" I say defeated getting off her lap.

"I see I've got a very sassy little one on my hands." She says shaking her head.

Nine

Hanaina decided to give me a day to really consider this relationship but I already knew my answer. We have been texting back and forth so I told her my final decision over text but she wants me to tell her in person.

She's coming over to my place today since we haven't really seen eachother. She's been working nonstop today which annoys me because she didn't answer my messages quick enough. I'm sitting and waiting for her to come by. I have a tub of ice cream and youtube to help distract me from the anticipation.

I hear a knock and jump rushing to the door. I giggle peeking through the window to see if it's really her. She spots me putting her hands on her hips "open the door young lady." She says looking unpleased with me making her stand outside in the cold. I quickly open the door and she squeezes me in a tight hug.

"Why is there a big ice cream tub open? No none of that! Put it away it's cold enough outside." She's so mean, but I listen not wanting her to scold me anymore. After putting my ice cream away I join her on my wrecked couch.

"We have rules, punishments, rewards and boundaries to discuss." She says so casually patting my thigh. Punishments? Uh-uh "What's wrong pumpkin?" She asks reading my expression.

"Why punishments?" I ask whining.

"Because rules can't exist without punishments in place." I look away. I still don't like the idea of her punishing me. I've never really gotten in trouble with her so I wonder what she's going to say.

"Alright rules first." She looks at me for approval. I respond with a nod. "These apply immediately once you consent to this dynamic".

"Firsty I will be addressed as Mommy, Mama or Mom, this applies while you're big or small. I better not hear 'Hanaina' come out your mouth." She sounds really stern so I just nod.

"You are to eat three meals a day with snacks in between. I'm not too worried about your food intake though, you eat just fine." I smile proud of myself. "Well...when I'm around." she says making my smile drop.

"Three, you are to tell the truth, you're not too good with lying, so I'm also not worried about that." I look away embarrassed by her statement. I mean that's a good thing right? Right?!

I never really lie, my dad wouldn't believe me even when I told the truth. He would punch me even when I was telling the truth and claim I was lying. I still wonder why he felt I was incapable of being honest. I think I started lying anyway because he would hurt me whether I told the truth or not.

"Nollani? Are you Alright?" I nod focusing on her again.

"Okay, I was saying you need to tell me if there's something going on in that head. If something is bothering you, it's better to talk to me than to keep it all in there" She says booping my nose. I smile at her sudden action. "If you're unhappy with mommy, you tell me so we can reach a common ground." I nod.

"Always use your words. I'm can't read minds so I need you to use your words."

"I will be informed about your whereabouts and you are to be back before your curfew, unless we've discussed otherwise. With that being said curfew is a 10pm nothing later than that." That's not even a rule, I'm always home.

"Bedtime is at 9pm, besides Fridays and Saturdays. No argument." I'm used to sleeping after midnight it's way more fun too. I only slept at 9 when I had to wake up to go to her office. That wasn't very nice.

"We are responsible for our own mess, you make a mess you are to clean it up. Unless you really need my help, which I predict you will." She says looking at the blob of chocolate ice cream on my shirt. Hey! When did that get there?

"No sweet things before bedtime or in the morning." boring! "Also I don't want you having coffee" what the hell! This is really stupid!

"No cursing." She says sounding veeery serious.

"No using dangerous objects while I'm not around."

"No drinking alcoholic beverages unless I'm around and know about it." I don't really drink so that isn't much of a challenge.

"Finally, always listen to mommy!" She says stressing the word always. "Should I feel or if you feel that a rule should be added then we will discuss that. Now punishments and rewards."

Ohhhh shit!

"Alright, so if you're a very good girl you get a sticker on your progress chart. Each sticker is an achievement but if you have 5 - 7 stickers by the end of the week then you can choose to get a new stuffy or ask mommy for anything you might want at the time." I smirk knowing she's is gonna be bankrupt after all my rewards.

"There's going to be a small reward for 5 stickers by the end of the week, a better one for 6 stickers and obviously a big reward if you get 7 stickers." I nod, I'm so excited!

"Now punishments." She glances at me for a second before she continues "Punishments would typically be some time in the corner, lines and spankings. Nothing too much." I furrow my eyebrows, nothing too much? "Use your words please."

"Spankings hurt and lines make my hands hurt and timeout is boring!" I say whining and crossing my arms over my chest.

"They're supposed to bubba, if you stay out of trouble then you don't have to worry about anything hurting or anything being boring." I pout at her not very pleased.

"Now it's time for boundaries, did you do the homework I asked you to do?" She asks.

"Homework?" I ask confused.

"Nollani, I remember asking you very nicely to write down your boundaries so we can discuss them together." She states staring at me with her dark eyes. I shrink under her gaze. I completely forgot to do that but I know them in my head.

"I forgot Miss Hanaina but I know them by heart." I say trying my luck. Now she probably thinks I'm bad. I notice her wrinkling her nose at me calling her by name but she doesn't say anything about it.

"Hmm, I'm letting this one slide, but next time there will be trouble if I give you something to do and you don't do it." She says fixing her glasses still staring daggers as me. "Am I clear?"

"Yes mo- ma'am." I shake my head at my little mistake. I don't think she noticed though because she didn't react to it.

"Go ahead pumpkin. Boundaries"

"Okay, no lines, corner time or spankings" she raises an eyebrow obviously unpleased. "and I don't want anything s-sexual while I'm big or small." I whisper the last part. She nods before speaking.

"You are acting smart with me and it's not gonna work. Lines, timeout and spankings still stand. You're going to be my baby so sexual activities are fully prohibited from my side as well." She states simply. "Is that all?"

I nod looking away unable to think of anything else.

"Are you comfortable with me seeing you undressed? For bath time or to change you?" I blush not expecting that question. I can change my own clothes and bath on my own but I nod my head anyway. I don't mind her being my peasant. "Words!" She says with her mommy voice.

"Yes." I say not looking at her.

"Okay final question, do you consent to me being your mommy and carrying out my duties as your mommy? I would like you to use your words this time please."

"Yes Miss Hanaina" I say practically screaming with excitement. She laughs engulfing me in the best hug ever.

"My baby." She whispers into my ear, kissing my cheek.

Ten

I've finally moved in with Hanaina, it's my first full day with her. She's been to the office these past few days while my items were delivered to her house bit by bit. She was supposed to go to the office today but she decided to stay just to show me around the house and help me settle in.

I've told Hafsa and Aunty Jasmines that I finally took Hanaina's offer to live with her instead of alone. Hafsa made fun of me initially saying I chose to live with the strictest person alive than to live with her 'chilled' mom. She said we could've practically been siblings. Typical for Hafsa to say.

Hanaina is sweet to me, sure she can be scary sometimes but she's been nice to me. I haven't fully embraced this whole relationship, but then again with the whole moving in thing I hadn't gotten the chance to.

I can't get myself to call her mommy though. It's too foreign on my tongue. Maybe because I never got to spend time with my mom since my paternal grandmother raised me. I would visit my mother every school break and it was the best thing ever. My mother's side was way more fun. My mother passed away a few months before I turned 18 and it was never the same for me. I still remember how she made me feel so loved, I just miss her everyday.

"Nollani?"

"Yes?" I answer shaken out of my thoughts.

"Here baby let me show you around." she says appearing out of nowhere. We go upstairs and our first destination is a room at the end of the corridor. My room. The walls were painted in pastel colours. There was a big bed with white wooden rails on all four sides. Above the bed was a pastel pink coloured princess canopy.

The room had a big window with a window seat. On each side of the window were shelves that were decorated with books, vases and lots of stuffies. There was a big fluffy white mat with a basket of toys and a rocking chair placed on it. We were about to leave the room when I spotted a dresser that had a soft mat looking thing on it. I wonder what that's for.

I really liked the room. If it's pastel coloured, then it's a yes from me. I wanted to jump up and squealing with excitement but that was just embarrassing to do in front of Hanaina.

We move on to the other rooms including bathroom and Hanaina's office down the corridor. Hanaina's room is right next to my room at the very end of the corridor. That means I don't have to try too hard to look for her in this gigantic house.

After showing me her office, which I saw the first time I came here, she shows me the room opposite her office. My eyes go wide, it's heaven on earth. It's a play room, she said it's all for me. I wanna play now! My feet hurt already from just one corridor she should just let me stay here.

"Let me just show you the rest of the house." She says walking out the door but turns around when she notices I'm not following her. "Are you okay baby?" She asks.

"I'm tired now." I say determined to play here instead of walking around.

"Would you like me to hold you?" She asks holding out her hands.

"No me stay here, and rest. I tired. You see house alone." She looks at me before she chuckles.

"You wanna play here while I give myself a tour of my own house?" She asks with a smirk. "Nollani, you can come back here in a bit pumpkin then you can play all you want." I look away not wanting to admit that I actually wanna play and not rest.

"No mommy me not play, me jus resting ." She gasps. What? Did I hurt her feelings? "I play with you mommy?" I say trying to make her feel better. This time she smiles at me nodding her head. I knew mommy wanted to play here too. It looks so fun. She rubs each of her eyes, I wonder if something got in her eyes.

"Mommy eyes hurt?" She smiles sitting down on the floor taking me down into her lap. She gives me a tight cuddle and a kiss on the forehead. I take in her scent rubbing my face on her chest before going to grab a few toys to play with.

I don't know where to start there's just so much to do. I eventually settle on the big doll house giving mommy one of the dolls so she doesn't feel left out. I'm having the bestest fun when mommy interrupts me by pulling me onto her hip.

"No mommy me play." I say throwing myself backwards and squirming in her arms.

"Nollani! Behave." She gives me a scary mommy look making me hide my face in her neck.

"You can always play sweet girl but we need to get you and mommy something to eat. I promise to let you play after". I nod letting mommy carry me to the kitchen. I'm definitely going back there to play with more of the toys she can't stop me.

Eleven

Hanaina's Pov

I've decided to go to the office this morning. I've also decided to take nollani with because I don't want her to be alone incase she slips. I gently shake Nollani awake only receiving a smack on my arm before she turns away from me. Cheeky girl.

She slept with me last night because she didn't want to sleep in her own room but that was the least difficult part from last night. What tasseled me was getting her out of that play room to get her ready for bed, after a lot of convincing she finally agreed to get ready for bed.

Having Nollani around has been quite different from the last time I had a little one. Slipping wasn't as easy for my previous little, I really needed to put in some work to get her to be little. Nollani slips quite easily, like how she did when she saw the playroom. My previous little was more of an infant so Nollani being around 3 years old is different. I don't have a little age preference so I don't mind the change.

Nollani is way more comfortable around me when little. She's carefree and very stubborn while little. "Baby we have to get ready, I don't want to be late for work." I say trying to sit her up hoping that it's going to get her to wake up. It doesn't really work so I use a stern tone. "Nollani I'm going to start counting to three and if you're not up you're going to be in a lot of trouble."

"I'm up." She says rubbing the sleep out of her eyes. I let her use my bathroom to get ready while I get myself dressed. I know I'm not being the best mommy ever but we can pick up breakfast on the way to the office. It's only for today because I haven't worked out a proper morning routine that also accommodates Nollani.

I move into my office to grab a few documents before going downstairs. I hadn't picked out anything for Nollani to wear so I go back upstairs. "Oh!" I say in shock. I'm met with a naked Nollani tiptoeing to her room. She turns a bright shade of red, covering her non existent chest area and her princess part. I turn away from her so she doesn't feel more uncomfortable.

"Sorry pumpkin I was trying to get you some clothes. Should I still do so or are you going to do it yourself?" She's quiet for a few seconds.

"I'll do it" She says. I nod hearing her feet tapping on the floor followed by the door closing. I really need to work on a routine to avoid stupid mistakes like these. I even forgot to give her a towel, that poor baby.

"Miss Hanaina." She calls me, of course using my name.

"Yes?" I stand outside her door knocking lightly. She opens her door looking distressed.

"I need help with my hair please." I smile leading her to a her little white vanity. I notice her outfit, she looks so adorable.

"What would you like me to do?" She shrugs so I decide on two plaits. I gently brush through her hair parting it in the middle. I start with the plaits and give her a kiss on her head once I'm done. "All done pumpkin."

"Thank you." She smiles seeming happy with her hair.

"Alright put your shoes on and let's go. We'll grab breakfast on our way to the office. I go downstairs to get my car keys. I hop into the car and pull out of the garage. Nollani comes out a second later with her little backpack. She opens the door to the passenger seat. "No, little girls sit in the back."

"What but I'm big!"

"I know you're big but you're sitting in the back."

"That isn't fair." She says stomping her foot.

"I'm only going to speak once young lady." I say using my dominating voice. She slams the door. "Nollani!" She's so cheeky. She gets in the back putting her seat belt on before I could even tell her. I look in the rear view mirror and notice shes upset. I shake my head smiling at how adorable she looks when angry.

I get us breakfast sandwiches, a coffee for myself and a hot chocolate for her. That didn't go well because Nollani wanted coffee as well but that's not going to happen. She's been so cranky this morning, I've probably already grown a hundred grey hairs just from this morning.

We get to the office right on time. Little miss sassy goes to lay on the couch obviously not wanting to be anywhere near me. I let her be before getting a piece of paper and setting it next to me.

"Nollani could you come over here please." I say using my stern voice. She comes over with her arms folded over her chest not looking at me.

"I'm not happy with your behaviour this morning, you broke two rules and you've been very sassy." She starts playing with her fingers. "Can you tell me why you're so upset?" I ask gently.

"You made me sit in the back this morning and got me hot chocolate instead of coffee. I'm a big girl I can have coffee and I can sit in the front."

"No! You are my little girl so you will sit in the back and you are not allowed to have coffee." I respond very firmly.

"But that's not fair!" She whines. Latisha walks into the office sensing the tension in the room. I speak with Latish briefing her about what I expect from her. She reminds me about the meeting I have with HR before leaving the two of us in the room again.

"You do not stomp your foot at me. Incase you don't remember, one of the rules was to always listen to mommy. Something you're not doing right now." I pause looking at her seeing how nervous she looks. "You also happened to break the rule to call me mommy, mama or mom and not by my name." She gasps. Her cheeks turn red, a pretty frequent occurance.

She opens her mouth before closing it again. I can tell that she's finally given up her little attitude. "You're going to write 'I will listen to mommy and I will not call mommy by name'. You're going to write that on both sides of the page neat and no big handwriting. Am I understood? " I look at her with a raised eyebrow.

"Yes."

"Yes what?"

"Yes m-mommy." She says not looking at me.

"There we go, sit right next to me and start." She does as I say grabbing the pen and paper I placed in front of her. Now that's a good girl.

Twelve

I had fun in mommy's office today, not so much in the morning but the rest of the day was fun. Mommy put on Tinkerbell, my favourite. Tisha also let me play with her pretty long hair and even gave me an ice lollie while mommy was gone to a meeting. Mommy found out though because my dress was messy and Latisha got in trouble. Mommy's a party pooper!

As soon as mommy and I got home I made her chase me around the house. I took away the knife she was using to chop up yucky onions and ran away with it. It was so fun but mommy caught me, bent me over her arm and smacked my bum three times really hard. Mommy's such a party pooper.

"I don't know how you went from being shy to being so naughty!" She said making me whine into her chest. I poked her nose and she tried to bite my finger but I quickly hid it from her.

When mommy finished cooking she sat me at the table right next to her and put a bib around my neck. I'm not a baby so I gave mommy a scary face! Mommy ignored me and gave me a pretty plastic plate with chicken tendies and creamy pasta. I look at mommy's plate and she also had creamy pasta but hers looked way more yummy. Mommy hands me a pretty cup with juice so I make a happy dance.

She finally sits down next to me and starts to eat her food. I grab my chicken tendie and eat it along with some of mommy's pasta. "Yummy mommy!" I say wiggling in my seat.

"I can see that." She says giving me another tendie. I feed some to mommy but she says she's already full. Once I'm done I get off my chair wanting to sit on mommy's lap. It was way more comfortable than this chair.

"You need a bath." Mommy says as he stands up carrying me on her hip. She grabs our plates and puts them in the sink. I lay my head on her shoulder enjoying the comfort. I'm really messy but mommy doesn't mind.

We get to my bathroom and mommy sits on the closed toilet running the water for me and adds a bath bomb. The water looked so pretty with glitter I had to get in. I jump off her lap quickly taking off my clothes. My dress got stuck over my head, making me whine because it's all dark and scary.

"You're fine! Here, mommy help you." mommy says sounding like a baby. It's bright again so I let mommy take off the rest of my clothes. She saw me nakey this morning anyway so I don't care. Mommy picks me up setting me in the water. She leaves for a few seconds and comes back with a big fluffy purple froggy towel.

"Mommy you wanna play too?" I ask her as she puts some toys into my water.

"No sweetheart you can play while mommy cleans you up." I play letting mommy do her thing. I'm having a lot of fun and only jump in surprise when mommy cleans my bum, I go back to playing a second later though knowing I can trust her. Mommy then let's me play for a while."Come baby we need to get you dressed, the water's gone cold."

"No mommy I still playing" She shakes her head pulling me out of the water anyway. Stupid strong mommy I pout. She kisses my pouted lips making my cheeks warm.

"Aww is the baby shy now?" She asks putting some lotion on me. I hide my face with my hands.

"Mommy stop it, not a baby!" I cry out in frustration. She chuckles picking me up and taking me to my room. She places me on the big soft mat on the dresser, the one I saw yesterday. She works quickly getting me dressed and puts something rubbery in my mouth. A binky! I've never had one before. I like it but not as much as my fingers, I won't tell mommy that though.

Mommy gets me dressed in a green Tinkerbell nightie and white socks. Once she sets me on my feet I twirl around on my tippy toes with my arms up like a ballerina.

"Let's get you a bottle sweet girl, I'm sure you're a bit thirsty." I run off leaving mommy behind.

"Nollani!" Mommy shouts making me stop right at the top of the stairs. Mommy comes and I hold onto her hand so I don't fall down the stairs. They're so much higher than I remember, they look so scary. I sigh a sigh of relief once we get to the bottom of them. Mommy puts the TV on for me before going into the kitchen.

She comes back out and sits me on her lap. Where's my bottle of water I'm really thirsty now. Mommy pulls out a bottle of milk instead. "Mommy no! No milk, water!" I say trying to get off her lap but she's just too strong.

"Try it and then if you don't like it mommy's going to give you your water." Mommy says pulling the binky out, holding the bottle to my lips. I turn away with my mouth shut. Mommy holds my nose and shoves the bottle in my mouth when I gasp for air. I look up at mommy not very pleased.

I try it like she says. I suckle and yummy milk fills my mouth. I suckle some more and mommy pulls the bottle out my mouth. I groan looking at her. "You need to slow down baby, be gentle, the milk is all yours." Mommy says and sticks the bottle back in my mouth letting me hold my own bottle. This time I listen to mommy enjoying every bit of the milk. Way better than water.

I smile looking up at mommy, playing with her hair. My eyes start to feel heavy, I'm not sleepy though. Mommy gently brushes my eyebrows with her finger making my eyes more heavy. I let her carry on because it feels good. Mommy's heartbeat isn't helping the situation so I decide to close my eyes letting mommy hold my bottle up for me again.

I feel safe and peaceful. I finally fall asleep cuddled up against my mommy.

Thirteen

I wake up to the bed shaking. I open my eyes and it's Han- mommy shaking me awake. Could she just let me sleep, just for today. Ha-um-mommy pulls the blanket off and I shiver. It's unusually cold.

"Sweetheart, did you have an accident?" She asks looking down at my legs. I sit up trying to see what she looking at. I freeze feeling the wetness from the slight movement. I look at her trying to see if she's angry but she softly smiles at me.

"I'm sorry." I say looking away.

"I gave you a full bottle last night it was bound to happen. Are you big right now?" She asks which I respond with a nod. "Could you please get ready for me while I change your bed sheets? Just put your wet clothes in the laundry basket I'll sort it out." I nod again wondering how she's still so sweet to me when I'm giving her extra work early in the morning.

While I'm taking a bath, I hear a knock at the door. "Come in." I say not worried about her seeing me naked. I look up at her still embarrassed about my accident. I haven't had an accident in ages, why now? I usually hold my pee in all night too scared to go to the bathroom so it really surprises me how I had an accident.

"It's okay sweetheart mistakes like that happen. I should've put you in some sort of protection instead of panties. Anyway would you like me to pick out your clothes or will you do it yourself?" She asks. I look at her longer than I should be. I really can't help it she looks so beautiful. I don't understand how she makes work clothes look so good. "Nollani!" She snaps me back to reality.

"You look beautiful mommy." I smile at her.

"Thank you sweetheart, but you still haven't answered me." She says waiting for an answer.

"Can you please pick them out." I say.

"Alright. Well done for using your manners." she says making me flush. I'm not used to all this praising. She's doing it on purpose, I'll definitely get her back.

Once I'm done I go to my room to get ready. I see my clothes laid neatly on the bed. Lo and behold we're matching. She picked out a white long sleeved tshirt with baby blue ruffled shorts.

Incase I hadn't mentioned it, she's wearing a baby blue pantsuit. Great a mini Hanaina! What are they gonna think when we get to the office. Even worse we'll be walking in together. I get dressed anyway. Never letting her pick my clothes again.

"Nollani! Let's go baby."

"Coming!" I call back. I quickly take my bag, secretly stuffing one of the sloth stuffies in and my binky in the pocket of my shorts. Why I decided to take them? I don't know but I had to bring them with. I run off downstairs into mommy's car. I don't even bother trying my luck and go straight to sitting at the back. Mommy had given me some pancakes with fruits to eat on the way.

We drive by the coffee shop, she gets me a hot chocolate again and gets herself a coffee. I fold my arms not taking it when she hands it to me. "Nollani, I'm not going to put up with this again. If you want to act like a baby then I have not issue treating you like one." She says firmly.

"That's not fair!" I shake my head not giving in.

"Fine then." She says placing the hot chocolate in the cup holder. I smile knowing I won this time. She quietly drives off, drinking some of her coffee. The hot chocolate smells so good so I end up drinking it. It's not my proudest moment but whatever.

She places her coffee in the cup holder. I eye it for a bit so temped to take it but I know better than to get in trouble in the morning...again.

When we arrive, I jump out the car closing the door walking a little ahead of her. I'm still upset about the coffee and it's pretty clear to see. I notice some of the staff looking at us which makes me very conscious. I look back a mommy wanting a bit of reassurance. She's walking behind me not paying anyone any attention and that makes me confident enough. I get on the elevator, holding the door open because I'm kind. She thanks me and presses the button to our floor.

As soon as the door opens again I run off to our office, dumping my bag on the couch. I'm about to run off to Latisha's office which is right next door, but bump into mommy. "Where are you going?"

"I wanna spend some time with Tisha. Please!" I say with my best puppy eyes.

She sets her stuff before sitting on her chair and waves for me to come closer. I stand next to her not knowing what to expect. "You can go sit with Latisha but this coffee issue is not going to be a common occurance every morning. This is the last time you're going to throw a tantrum over coffee. Yes?"

"Yes Mommy."

"Good girl" she smiles waving her hand signalling me go on. I run off to Tisha's office.

"You're matching with my wife! She's mine!" Lydia says dramatically holding her forehead. Does She have nothing to do? She's literally always in here.

"Lydia shut up. You're always eye fucking the poor woman." Tisha says clicking her tongue.

"You're just jealous! Always keeping her to yourself." Lydia says with the funniest expression ever. "I stole her number off your phone yesterday" she says with a smirk.

"Lydia you bitch, you better not do anything. You'll freaking get me in trouble. Delete it now!" Tisha says trying to take Lydia's phone. Lydia shoves it in her bra and turns her back to Tisha. I giggle looking at them bickering. This is why I enjoy coming here. I wonder what mommy would say if she knew how silly these two act. Especially Tisha because she's always such an angel in front of mommy.

Speaking of mommy, I kinda miss her now. I leave these two digging in each other's bras for a stupid phone. I've had enough Lydia-Latisha dose for this morning.

"So soon?" Mommy asks without looking up.

"Can you smell me? I literally just walked in." I say in a bored tone shoving myself on her lap. She chuckles pinching my cheeks. I don't feel little but I just want to be near her.

"Whats wrong sweetie?" She asks cradling me.

"Shhh! Cuddle me mommy cuddle me!"

"Yes ma'am!" she says squishing me against her boobies making me whine.

"I said cuddle me mommy not kill me!" I tell her stern. She rudely laughs at me. Not funny!

"What's this bubba?" She asks feeling the lump in my pocket. I look up confused before remembering the binky in my pocket.

"No, nothing." I say, quickly covering my pocket with my hand.

"Nollani! What did I say about lying?" She says pulling my hand away and taking the binky out of my pocket. I hide my face in her chest in embarrassment. This day sure is going really well for me!

"Ohh sweetheart!" Mommy kisses me on the head. "You don't have to be embarrassed about your binky. I don't mind you using it whenever you want to." She says booping my nose.

I grab the binky from her hand sticking it in my mouth and going back in her chest. I don't want her to take my binky again. She chuckles rubbing my back.

"I wonder why Latisha hasn't come in here yet, I should probably ring her" mommy does so and Tisha comes in a few seconds later looking disheveled.

"What on earth happened to you?" Mommy says. I look up at mommy giggling knowingly. Ohh stupid Tisha.

Fourteen

It's been a really long week, I won't have to wake me up tomorrow morning, yay! I went to meet new people with mommy today. Mommy tried to make me stay with Tisha but I didn't want to stay with her I wanted my mommy. Mommy was talking to the strangers while I sat on her lap enjoying my binky. I don't know what was said but there was a lot of talking. I dosed off a few times but mommy kept waking me up.

I was currently watching Bluey on mommy's Ipad. Mommy set me on a blanket on the floor so I could colour while I watched Bluey. "Baby?" Mommy calls me, I look up at her. "Would you like a bottle before we leave?" Mommy asks mainly because I kept demanding for milky but mommy said I could have it a little later and she gave me a snack instead.

"Yes p'ease." I respond excited.

"I've asked Latisha to get you your babba, she'll be here in a bit" I go back to my colouring trying my hardest to be patient. Latisha walks in a while later handing my babba to Mommy and leaving the two of us alone again. I run over to Mommy climbing on her lap, wasn't easy but mommy helped me up. I snatch my babba away and quickly suckle. I remember to be more gentle so Mommy doesn't to take it away.

When my milky is all finished I hand mommy the bottle. I still wanted more but I didn't want to ask mommy, I think I nagged her enough for milky today. Mommy positions me so that I'm straddling her lap and I lay my head on her chest listening to her heartbeat.

"Mommy Lydia have a crush on you." I say after some time of sitting in Silence. I need something to keep me awake and Lydia's crush on my mommy was good enough.

"What? Who's Lydia? Mommy asks confused.

"Tisha friend, she say she want you to step on her." Mommy gasps. "But Lydia get a ouchie if mommy step on her." I say looking up and Mommy looks distraught.

"What's her name?" She asks me.

"Her Lydia mommy!" I say like it's the most obvious thing ever.

"Lydia works here?" She doesn't know her own employees?

"Yes, her work here"

"Hmm." Mommy hums bouncing me on her lap. I know mommy is trying to get me to sleep but I still wanna ask her questions.

"You have a boyfriend?" I ask mommy.

"No I do not! You need to close your eyes and sleep." She replies bouncing me even harder. When I wanted to sleep she didn't let me, now when I don't want to sleep she forces me to sleep!

"How old are you Mommy?" Mommy looks at me contemplating whether she should tell me or not.

"If I tell you do you promise to sleep?" Now I look at Mommy not sure whether I should promise or not, I don't really have to keep my promise though.

"P'omise!" I say with my fingers crossed behind my back.

"Mommy is 38 years old, now your promise!" Mommy says pushing my head on her chest not letting me lift it up. The good part is that her boobies are really soft so I let her hold me against her chest.

"Mommy?"

"Yes baby?" Mommy responds sounding fed up.

"Your boobies have milky?" I ask making Mommy choke on her spit. She lifts my chin up making me look at her. She looks very serious, maybe I overstepped.

I look at Mommy waiting for her to scold me for asking her that question. "I know I didn't tell you but you liked it so I let you have it." I look at mommy completely blank. What does she mean. She sees my confusion. " Baby, the milk in your babba is from mommy. I gave it to you just to see if you'd like it and you did, so I let you have it." I have no idea how to respond.

"But Tisha made my babba!" I say trying to understand how my milky was from mommy if Tisha gave mommy my babba just now.

Mommy shakes her head. "I had put it in your bottle this morning, I just asked Tisha to warm it up for me because I left it in the fridge when we got to the office." I looked away from mommy's face now to her chest. Is that why her boobies look so big? I want the milky right now but I'm too afraid to ask so I lay on mommy's chest hoping she'll read my mind.

"Does that bother you sweet girl? I can stop giving you my milk if you're not comfortable." Mommy says scratching my back. I shake my head hiding in her chest.

"Mommy milky yummy!" I say softly not looking up at her. It's a bit embarrassing that I had her milky and shamelessly enjoyed it. "Your other baby have your milky?" I ask curious.

"She was way younger than you so she mostly had my milky." I huff in anger making Mommy lift my chin up again, to meet her gaze.

"What is it pumpkin? Tell mommy."

"You mine, my mommy" I say. "Is my milky not hers." I pout not happy about someone else having my milky.

"I know pumpkin, but you asked and I gave you an honest response. You're so possessive." She says giving me a kiss on the lips. My pout completely disappears, I use my hands to hide my smile.

"I no like her having my milky!" I tell mommy.

"That's what happens when mommy tells you to sleep but you chose to be cheeky and talk about my boobies and Lydia." I giggle hearing mommy saying the word boobies.

"Sleeping is boring, me wanna talk." I say proudly.

"I see that. Mommy's ears are gonna fall off. So talkative!"

"Not talkative! But why Lydia want mommy to step on her?" Mommy gasps looking at me stern.

"That's enough!" Mommy says scolding me. "Let's go home. You need a bit of an afternoon N-A-P" Mommy says standing up with me on her hip I'm very excited to go home, not sure what "N-A-P" is though.

Fifteen

I woke mommy up this morning just to level things between us. It's not really revenge but she needs a taste of her own medicine. She gave me breakfast and a bath then I decided to spend some time in the playroom but got bored after a while. I don't know where mommy is, so I decide to have fun with her make up.

I tippy toe to her room carefully opening the door. Mommy's doors don't creak and squeak so that makes things easier for me. I look around the room trying to see if mommy's in there. She isn't in the room so I quickly go in the bathroom opening the cabinet looking for her make up stash. I wiggle happily once I find it.

"What are you doing?" Mommy asks startling me.

I look up seeing mommy nakey wiping herself dry with a towel. How didn't I see her? I look at Mommy frozen in place, blushing when my eyes go down to her boobies. I quickly throw the items in my hands back in the cupboard running out of the room before mommy could say anything.

I've never seen mommy nakey before. Seeing her nakey only made my desire to have milky from her increase. I sit behind the door in my playroom hoping mommy doesn't find me. I start feeling drowsy from sitting behind the door. My eyes shoot open when I feel myself getting picked up.

"That's why you should've listened to me when I told you to go back to sleep this morning." Mommy says making me huff. We're in my room and mommy puts me on the big fluffy mat that's on my dresser. I frown when she takes my undies off and putting on something fluffy under my bum.

When I try to see what it is, mommy pushes me back down before picking me up again. "It's a diaper pumpkin, it's best if we keep it on just to be safe." I whine not happy that she put me in a stupid diaper.

"I'm not a baby!" I say folding my arms. Mommy ignores me and sits on the rocking chair. She pats my bottom which makes me squirm in her lap. I don't like how the diaper makes a thud noise every time mommy pats my bum.

When mommy tries to put the binky in my mouth I hide in her chest. I didn't want a binky I wanted her boobies. Mommy tries again but this time I take it and throw it across the room. "Nollani! That was not very nice." I ignore mommy determined to get my milky.

I lay against mommy deciding to get the milky myself since she doesn't wanna give it to me. I put my hand down her shirt reaching for one of mommy's boobies. Mommy doesn't say anything watching me quietly. When I fail to pull her boobie out, I groan in frustration kicking my legs.

I regret my actions as soon as I look up at mommy. I hide behind my hands hoping she can't see me anymore. "What is it that you want baby tell mommy." Mommy asks gently rubbing circles on my cheek. I shake my head deciding it's best to close my eyes and sleep.

After a while of nothing but silence I feel something pressed on my mouth. I open my mouth this time deciding it's best to just have my binky. I realise it's not my binky because it's way too soft. I open my eyes seeing mommy's boobie in my mouth instead. I look up at mommy trying to read her expression but she nods encouraging me to suckle.

I suckle and my head feels so fuzzy from a lot of emotions. I tug on mommy's boobie wanting more milk but it only slows down. I huff asking mommy for help with my eyes. "Gently baby, gently" I do as she says recieveing a "Good girl." She adjusts me, and milk suddenly fills my mouth. I tastes just like the one from my babba maybe a little bit better.

Mommy continues patting my bum. My eyes feel so heavy but I have to stay awake, I want to have more of mommy's milky. I can't keep them open anymore, leting sleep envelope me.

I wake up to a lot of noise. I realise I'm in my room so it's mommy making noise. Why does mommy have the TV on so loud. I slowly get off the bed so I don't fall off, that would really hurt. I go down the stairs scooting on my bum. I reach the bottom looking up to lots of eyes looking back at me. I run in the direction of the only familiar pair of eyes I see.

Mommy grunts catching me in her arms. I sit curled into her not wanting to look at the 2 women sitting in front of us. "Baby what happened to our manners? Can you say hi?" Mommy asks rubbing my back.

"Hi." I say still hiding.

"Hi sweetheart." One of the women says rubbing my foot. I peek trying to get a better view of these women. They both seem to be around mommy's age.

There's one that looks very kind and smiles at me when she catches me peeking. She has long dark wavy hair and pretty green eyes, she's wearing glasses like my mommy, except her glasses were sparkly, way prettier than mommy's boring ones. The other lady looks pretty but scary. She has brown hair that sits just above her shoulders and grey eyes. I wonder who they are.

It's as if mommy reads my mind because she introduces them to me. "Baby this is Elaina-" She gestures towards the one with the brown hair, "-and Alana, Ela's wife." She points at the one with wavy hair. "They're mommy's friends" Mommy says and they wave at me.

"Lana, Ela, this is Nollani." Mommy introduces me planting a kiss on my temple.

"Nice to finally meet you in person sweetheart. Your mommy told me how naughty you were this morning." Aunty Alana says making me glare at mommy. I wasn't being naughty this morning.

I squirm away from mommy's hand when she squishes my bum. "Mommy no!" I tell her not impressed with her actions.

"Calm down, mommy's just checking if you're still dry." I blush groaning when she sticks her finger peeking into my diaper. "Okay I'm done, you're dry. Mommy was just double checking." I shake my head folding my arms.

"Woke me up!" I tell mommy very upset with her.

"I'm sorry lovebug, Aunty Ela and Lana invited themselves over." Mommy says staring at the two women.

"Well we wouldn't have if your mommy had the curtesy to do it herself sweetie." Aunty Ela responds staring at mommy. Mommy looks like shes about to fight Aunty Ela so I decided to safely get off her lap and hide behind the couch.

Nothing ends up happening. Boring! So I decide to climb on the couch, mommy grabs my leg when she sees me wobbling. "Get down, you're going to get hurt."

"Won't mommy! Let go!" As soon as I pry her hands off I wobble even more losing my balance. It really hurts so I let out a loud wail. Mommy picks me up, rubbing some of the sore parts of my body.

"Ohh my baby!" Mommy says rocking me. Once I calm, mommy gives looks at me sternly. "Are we going to listen to mommy next time?" She asks.

"Yes mommy." I say wiping my tears and snot on her shirt.

"Looks like you made your mommy's boring shirt way more pretty." Lana says laughing. Mommy gives her a glare before they go back to their boring conversation, I wanna climb on the couch again so I attempt to.

"I'm going to smack you!" Mommy says with her teeth clenched making me sit immediately on her lap. I see disapproving looks from the women in front of me and hide my face.

"I think we might have found Rylie's partner in crime." Lana says looking between mommy and Aunty Elaina.

"No, Rylie is a on another different level of naughty." Mommy says shaking her head. "I wonder how you two are still in one piece. She such a sweetheart for me though"

"Which makes me wonder what you did to my baby because she listens to you." Ela says. Mommy smiles at the two women.

"It's my secret!" Mommy sats winking. Who the heck is Rylie? Why is my mommy calling her a sweetheart?"

"Who Rylie?" I ask looking between the three of them.

"Just like how you're my baby, Rylie's Lana and Ela's baby. I don't know why these two didn't bring her with." Mommy says. "You should've brought her and left yourselves at home."

"Uh-uh Mommy, be nice!" I tell mommy waging my finger at her.

"Yes ma'am" mommy says with a smirk. I nod in approval. She chuckles giving me a kiss.

"I go play pease?" I ask giving mommy my best puppy eyes.

"If you promise to clean up your toys because I did it alone last night." Mommy tells me lifting a brow.

"I pomise mommy" she nods tapping by bottom. I'm gonna have to get this diaper off. It's so annoying!

Sixteen

When I get to the playroom my first mission is to take this diaper off. I lift up my dress undoing the tabs on each side. I take the diaper off deciding to put it under my bed so mommy doesn't find it.

I walk back to my playroom but remember that mommy's downstairs with Aunty Ela and Lana so I can probably do some exploring. I decided it won't be anything that belongs in mommy's room, maybe her office. I look through mommy's things but I don't see anything interesting.

I grab a few pens from mommy's table deciding to make use of her boring papers. All the papers I find have lots of words on them so It's better if I just draw over the words. I'll make a picture for mommy. I draw the first picture but I don't like the way it looks and decide to take a different paper.

This one has a lot of words on it and a circle that looks like it's cut up into unequal pizza slices with numbers inside. The pizza looks plain so I decide to draw topping on it. I bounce on each foot. Something feels weird but it feels much better when I'm bouncing on my feet.

"Nollani? I've been calling you-" I hear mommy say down the passage.

"Mommy I in here" I say. I hear mommy's shoes on the floor and it sounds like she's walking very fast.

"What on earth are you doing in my office?!" Mommy asks looking pretty angry. I decide to show her the pizza I made for her. She can't get angry after seeing pizza, can she?

"Pizza mommy. Look!" Mommy takes her glasses off rubbing her eyes. Does mommy not like my drawing? "Mommy not like it?" I ask a bit heartbroken.

"Baby, it's not that mommy doesn't like it, those were mommy's very important documents. Mommy's working on something very important. Those documents are very important lovebug." My heart sinks, I can't believe how stupid I am.

"I sorry mommy, I fix it, p'omise." Mommy smiles reaching out for me. I put up my arms letting mommy pick me up. She sits on her chair with me facing her.

"It's not your fault, next time mommy would appreciate it if you don't touch anything on in her office. If you would like to make a pretty picture for monmy, like this one," mommy points at the pizza, "then you ask mommy for paper and I will happily give you some." I nod laying on mommy's chest.

Mommy suddenly lifts my dress up and lowers it again. I'm confused for a bit before realisation hits me. I blush looking up at mommy. "You could've at least put big girl panties on." I hide my face certain I'm beet red.

"Did you make a pee pee in your diaper?" Mommy asks. I quickly shake my head no, but now that mommy ask, I feel pressure in my bladder. Now it makes sense why I was bouncing on my feet earlier. I wiggle around in mommy's lap not sure how to tell her I need to go pee pee. I can't even press my legs together because of the way I'm sitting on her lap.

"Mommy called you multiple times, Aunty Ela and Aunty Lana really wanted to say bye, but someone was very busy in her mommy's office." I whine bouncing on mommy's lap.

"Mommy down! Now!" I say, but mommy doesn't sense the urgency so I hide my face and just let it go right on mommy's lap. Mommy gasps and her body feels so stiff. I feel tears burning my eyes. I'm pretty disappointed in myself, I can't even control myself anymore. "I sorry mommy." I say through my crys.

Mommy stands up going somewhere, I don't bother looking up. Mommy sets me on my feet pulling my dress over my head. I'm not paying much attention but mommy picks me up again and I feel water on my skin. I finally look up, seeing mommy nakey, standing in her shower.

My crying stops, now enjoying the warmth from the water and from mommy's skin. "All better?" Mommy asks running her fingers through my wet hair. I nod putting my fingers in my mouth.

After a while, mommy works quickly washing the both of us. She steps out the shower wraping us in a towel. When mommy tries to put me down I whine clinging to her, after multiple attempts to set me on my feet she finally gives up.

Mommy gets me dressed in a pretty dress but puts on another diaper on me. I frown at her not very happy. We go back to her room where she gets dressed while I wait for her on the bed. I see my binky on her bedside table putting it to use.

Mommy lays on the bed pulling me on top of her. "Do you want me to feed you?" She asks pulling my binky out of my mouth.

I look at mommy's boobies before shaking my head quickly saying "no thank you". My cheeks feel warm, having my milky from her is still a bit embarrassing.

I roll over, laying next to her. She grabs her phone doing something on it. Probably work because that's the only thing mommy ever does.

"No it is not work young lady!" I smile looking at her sheepishly. I need to work on this thinking out loud thing, it's not cool.

"Is so, mommy always doing boring work!"

"Not I do not!" I giggle at her little tantrum. I try to peak and see what she's doing on her phone. What could possibly be more entertaining than me. "Stop being so nosey." She says hiding her phone against her chest. When Mommy picks up her phone again, it upsets me.

"Mommy no phone!" I whine throwing my legs on the bed. I put my face in the pillow kneeling with my butt in the air. I take my binky from her sticking it back in my mouth. Now I don't want to talk to her anymore.

"Okay bubs, mommy's all yours" she says and I ignore her.

I feel her get off the bed but continue hiding my face. I feel myself getting pulled towards mommy and squeal trying to get away but it's already too late and she's already holding me. I look at Mommy trying to look stern like her when she's angry. That doesn't work because mommy kisses me on my binky making me smile.

"There she is." Mommy says smiling back at me. I lay on her shoulder accepting my defeat. "Food?" She asks and I wiggle excitedly making mommy chuckle.

Seventeen

"Tell her you'll be back by 5pm!"

"Okay Fine! I'll call you back"

If I'm being honest Hafsa is a very bad influence, I know she's up to something. She said to ask mommy to come over to her place. I didn't want to leave mommy alone but Hafsa is insisting I come. I head to mommy's office hoping I can convince her to let me go over to Hafsa's.

"Mommy?" I enter her office.

"Hmm" she looks up at me.

"Can you take me to Hafsa's place like right now, she'll bring me back in the afternoon." I'm really nervous. I cross my fingers waiting for her to respond.

"What time in the afternoon?"

"Around 5?"

"Are you asking or telling me?" She looks at me suspicious.

"Telling you." She nods, is that a yes or what?

"Okay I'll be right there, just a few seconds." I leave her office. I quickly tell Hafsa I'm coming over. They live like 30 minutes away which makes me dread the drive there.

During the drive mommy looks at me through the rear view mirror. I glance at her smiling. I think she knows I'm up to something but she's quiet about it. Well I'm not up to something, Hafsa is.

When we get there mommy comes in with me to say hi to Aunty yas and leaves after giving me a kiss and telling me to behave. We go up to Hafsa's room and she pulls out a bottle of vodka.

"Hafsa what the fuck! You called me over for a bottle of vodka?" I ask annoyed.

"Shut up!" She says covering my mouth! "We're going to take a few shots and then we'll put it away. I think about it for a few seconds and decide a few shots won't hurt.

"Fine, only a few shots" I tell her very serious. She quickly places 2 shot glasses on her bedside table and pours vodka in them. Incase you were wondering, this vodka is her dad's and so are these glasses. This girl is insane.

We both take our first shot and its too much for me. "I can't do another one it burns!" I tell her.

"Keep it down or mumma is going to hear you!" She says trying to pour more into the now empty glasses.

"Hear what?" Aunty Jas walks into the room. Hafsa fumbles and drops the bottle breaking it. The room immediately smells of Vodka stinging my nose. "Girls?" She looks at the two of us completely shocked.

She walks out of the room not saying a word. "You got us in shit!" I tell Hafsa panicking.

"You were the one being too loud she wouldn't have come in here!" How is she blaming me? The alcohol was her idea, her mother heard her telling me to be quiet. It's not my fault at all.

"We have to clean this up!" I tell Hafsa going to pick up pieces of glass. She helps with wiping the whole whole mess. Once we're done the two of us sit in complete silence before Aunty Jas comes in again.

"Lani, Hanaina's here to get you." She says not seeming upset with me. She leans on the door waiting for me to go and follows behind me. I see mommys car outside and guilt washes over me. I leave too afraid to even say bye to Aunty Jas. My head is slightly spinning and it was just one shot.

Mommy walks out the car coming over to my side. She doesn't say anything but opens the door for me and puts my seatbelt on. I look up at her about to say sorry but she closes the door. She goes into the driver's seat and sits for a few seconds before driving.

"Mommy?" I call her because I can't stand this silence.

"Yes?" She answers quietly.

"I'm sorry for what I did today." I tell her squirming in my seat. She doesn't respond which drives me crazy. I wish I didn't give into Hafsa's stupidity.

It feels like we've been driving for eternity. Mommy pulls onto the driveway walking inside. I slowly follow behind her, my head seems fine now but my nerves are through the roof.

She pulls out one of the chairs from the dining "Come here please." She says sitting on the chair. I walk over to her not wanting to anger her further and she sits me on her lap.

"Look at me please." I look up but fail to keep eye contact. She holds my chin up so now I have no option but to look at her. "What you and Hafsa did today was very naughty. I specifically told you to inform me if you wanted to drink and make sure I'm around to supervise you. You didn't do any of that." I wiggle around on her lap wanting to get off and run away.

"I'm sorry." I say blushing.

"I know you are baby, but I don't take issues regarding alcohol lighty. Especially if you slip while drunk and mommy's not around. That wouldn't have ended well." Mommy says looking very disappointed. My cheeks feel so warm from embarrassment.

"You are going to go over my knee. I know it's embarrassing but that blush on your cheeks isn't as close to the colour I'm going to turn your little bum." She says and quickly stands me next to her.

"Mommy no! I'll never do-" Before I could even finish she puts me over her lap lifting up my dress. This is such an awkward position, just staring at the floor. It's right now that I wish I had slipped, I probably wouldn't be as embarrassed as I am right now.

"Since it's your first serious offence, I'll go easy on you." She says before landing a hard smack on my bum. It immediately sets my bum on fire because I've never gotten spanked before.

"Why are you getting spanked?" She asks.

"Because I had alcohol in your absence and didn't inform you either." I tell her with a lump in my throat.

"That's right." She follows with the next smack and I can't help but reach back.

"No young lady. Remove that hand." Mommy says quickly pinning my hand on my back. She starts showering my poor bum with quick hard smacks. By the time she stops I'm a mess. I'm about to get off her lap but she pushes me back down pulling my panties off. "We only end spankings on the bare bottom. A few more then mommy's all done sweetheart."

I feel my whole world tumbling down, I don't think I can take anymore of this but have no choice at this point. I hear mommy landing a smack and my bum feels numb. It's only a second late that I feel it and I really want out right now. "Mommy no! No more, I sorry mommy!" I cry kicking my legs around.

"Is this going to happen again?" She asks still smacking my butt.

"No! P'omise" I say feeling myself slipping into little space.

"Five more sweet girl." She says rubbing my bottom.

Those five smacks feel like a million more. She finally stops and this time mommy really stops. I'm now laying limp over her lap completely exhausted. She picks me up laying my head on her chest whispering sweet things. "It's all done baby. All done. Mommy loves you so much." Mommy says giving me a kiss.

"Hurts mommy." I say rubbing my sore bum.

"I know sweetie mommy's going to apply something to make it better. You did so good." "Mommy milky?" I ask looking up at mommy. Mommy nods helping me latch on. Turns out a few shots of Vodka do hurt after all.

Eighteen

Hanaina's Pov

This morning has been very rough for the both of us. Nollani's back to attending classes which she isn't very happy about. She's been crying on and off all morning probably due to separation anxiety. I managed to get her in the car so I can drive her to school. What breaks me is how she hasn't spoken a word nor has she looked in my direction.

"Baby we're here, mommy will be here to get you when you're done." She doesn't budge and continues staring out the window. "Baby?" I call her reaching back and gently tapping her knee. She finally looks at me looking so empty. I see tears well up in her eyes and it absolutely breaks me.

"Come here sweetpea, come talk to mommy." I say reaching my arms out. She lets out a few whimpers quickly sitting herself on my lap and burying her face in my chest. "I know baby" I say rubbing her back letting her cry.

"No wanna go to class mommy, me go with mommy." She says looking up at me. I don't know how to say no to this precious face. I plant a kiss on her forehead trying to figure out what to do in this situation.

"Pumpkin you can't go with mommy, you have to attend classes. Mommy's gonna be right here to pick you up later. You can call mommy on the phone whenever you wanna talk but you must attend." She shakes her head wailing even louder.

I'm so close to taking her to work with me but I have to prioritise her future. I need her to be big right now so she can better understand me. I wait for her to fully calm down before trying again to convince her. "Lani can you listen to mommy please." I wait a few seconds and she looks up at me. "Can you try your best to be big right now?"

"No!" She says not leaving any room for anything otherwise.

"Are you mommy's good girl?" She nods sticking her fingers in her mouth. "Can you be mommy's good girl and try to be big for mommy?" She lays her head on my chest closing her eyes. I'm not sure if she's trying to be big or choosing to ignore me but I wait for her patiently.

When she looks up at me again, she tries to get off my lap but I hold her in place. I see a blush forming on her cheeks, which I find so adorable. "Are you big now?" She nods acting all shy. "Can you tell me what's on your mind right now?"

"I don't want to be away from you. I can miss class just for today, I promise to attend tomorrow. Please mommy! I mean I'm late for my first class anyway!" She says shrugging her shoulders. I shake my head, seeing how she's trying to get cheeky.

"No bubs, but how about you go today then you can have mommy all to yourself later. Anything you want." I say knowing I'm going to probably regret it. "If you miss me you can call and we'll talk all you want, I promise my love."

"You really have to keep your promise mommy." she says putting her forehead against mine. I peck her lips.

"I promise baby."

She opens my drivers door getting down with my help. I grab her bag from the back handing it to her. I give her kisses all over her face receiving a "mommy stop, people are watching!" I chuckle.

"Get to class baby, I love you." I say. She walks off and my heart breaks, my poor baby. I put on some music to distract myself.

I get to the office and thankfully everyone appears to be working. I buzz Latisha just to see what my schedule looks like today "Morning Miss Zalda" I can see the confusion on her face when she doesn't see Nollani around.

"Morning, she's at school sweetie." I tell her.

"Oh" She responds looking disappointed. Sometimes I feel as if I have two babies. Latisha tends to acts like a child occasionally or does something that a child would usually do. She isn't a regressor though because I would've probably noticed, I've had her as my assistant for 3 years now. I get instances where I wanna put her in the naughty corner or sit her on my lap like how I want to do right now.

"I just wanted to know if there's anything important I need to deal with today?"

"No, there's nothing but there's a few things you need to approve for this tomorrow night's event. There's a few things the event coordinator wanted to discuss with you." I nod.

"Have you checked the ven-" I'm cut off by someone yelling Latisha's name like an idiot. I look at Latisha waiting for an explanation. My door slams open and I'm met with a girl with long blond hair. Her mouth drops open. I lift up my eyebrow looking at her then back at Latisha.

"Sorry Zalda" Latisha says pulling the girl away. I hear the girl say "you didn't tell me she was here!" doing a terrible job at whispering. I wonder who she is and why she's slamming doors and yelling in my office. Latisha comes back a few minutes later apologising once again.

"Who was that?" I ask not looking away from my laptop.

"It's Lydia, she works in the executive branch, she's one of the assistants there. I nod recalling the conversation I had with Nollani about Lydia. I continue discussing issues about the coming event deciding to deal with Lydia later.

After doing a lot of work I look at the time and it should be safe to get Nollani from school. I miss my baby so much, I just wanna hold her. I get my phone and car keys heading to my car. Thankfully it's not late in the day so I'm not getting stuck in any traffic. When I get to her college we spot eachother at the same time. She comes over to my door opening it and reaching up to me.

"Hi sweet girl!" I say seeing how excited she is to see me. I pick her up and she sits on my lap cuddling me. "How did it go?" I ask brushing her hair away from her face.

"It was shit!"

"Hey, you're gonna get in trouble!" I say stern. "Mommy missed you, you didn't even care to call me." I look at her pouting.

"I didn't want to make you worried mommy. Aaaand I was fine because Hafsa was there." I nod understanding how close they are with each other. I'm happy as long as she's happy.

"Lets go, mommy still has a few things to do at the office." I say giving her one more kiss before letting go.

Nineteen

Since mommy had promised to give me anything I want, I asked her to go to one of the shopping malls nearby. I'm currently not feeling small, but the toy store will still do. Mommy decideds to take us to a different store before going to the toy store, which upset me. That wasn't the only thing that upset me though, mommy also decided holding my hand was the best thing for me...something about running away from her and getting lost. So boring.

We go into 'mommy's shop', it looks so boring there's practically nothing mommy could want from here. I'm just following mommy cause she's holding my hand, but I don't want to be in this store. When I notice the isle mommy's taking us to, I feel my cheeks heat up. "Whose are those for?" I ask mommy when she picks up a pack of diapers.

"I think we both know who these are for, mommy didn't get enough last time. These should last you a month... or two?" She says picking up another pack.

"Fuck no!" I say folding my arms.

"You better stop cursing little miss." Mommy tells me firmly. She grabs my hand heading to the cash register. I don't even look up at the lady that works here, she obviously knows these diapers are for me but isn't making it obvious. Stupid mommy. I don't even want to get anything from the toy store anymore.

Jokes on me though because my mood does a full 360 degrees when I spot the toy store. "Mommy quick!" I say letting go of her hand. I look around the store unsure of where to start. I know I look so childish right now but I couldn't care less.

"Slow down pumpkin. You can take as long as you need, we're not in a hurry." I slow down listening to mommy. I see a shelf of sticker books and decide that would be a good starting point. I pick a book of stickers and move on to other items. Once my arms are full I go back to mommy to tell her I'm ready to go pay. Deep down I feel so guilty and greedy for grabbing all these things.

"Done." I say looking up hopefully at mommy. I really hope she allows me to take all these things because I like every single one of them.

"Oh my goodness, surely we aren't taking every one of those." I look down at my things trying to think which I should put back. I turn to put the colouring books away because I have some of those at home but mommy stops me."No no lovebug. Mommy doesn't mind you taking all of these things, but you better be a very good girl for me!"

I jump up excited dropping some of the mystery boxes I picked. Mommy shakes her head helping me carry some items. Mommy pays for my stuff without any fuss. We head to the car and it's already dark outside. I skip in front of mommy looking back now and again to make sure she's still there.

Mommy buys takeout on the way home since she didn't think cooking would be a good idea. When we get home we eat and go our separate ways, to get ready for bed. I take a quick shower and go downstairs after to watch something. I scroll through Netflix and eventually pick gossip girl.

I text my paternal grandmother telling her I'll visit on Wednesday or Thursday this week . I spoke to her earlier today, just wanting to know if she's doing well. It warmed my heart how excited she was to speak to me. I said I would go see her sometime during the week depending on my classes, I just didn't specify when.

I hadn't told mommy about my decision to go visit so I head to her room to tell her. She's still in the bathroom so I sit on her bed and wait. She eventually walks out giving me a wink snd goes to get herself dressed. I'm watching her getting ready just admiring her. I love being around her, I know I don't feel little but I still enjoy being around my mommy. I like the attention she gives me even when I'm big me. I always feel so loved, just like when my mother was still alive.

Mommy eventually joins me on her bed, she sits next to me and pulls me into her side. "What is it love?" She asks giving me a kiss on the head.

"I spoke to my gran and I wanted to go see her one of these days if that's okay with you?" I look up at her waiting for a response.

"I don't have an issue with that, you'll just tell me when and I'll take you. Are you planning to spend the night?" I nod.

"I can uber to-"

"Absolutely not! I'll get you in the morning and take you to school" typical of her! I nod once again not wanting to argue with her. "Would you like to sleep with me or in your room?" She asks. I'm feeling very big but her room sounds way better. Plus, I don't get nightmares when I sleep with her as opposed to when I sleep on my own.

"With you please." I say hoping she doesn't dislike my answer. She smiles softly giving me another kiss before picking me up to tuck me in under the covers. She gets in next to me moving very close to me. Her chest is practically in my face and I can't help but look at her cleavage.

"Staring is rude." She says smirking. I blush turning away to hide. I peek one last time. I would really like to nurse but I'm not feeling small so it wouldn't be appropriate.

"Nollani?" I quickly look away from her chest to her face. "If you want to have milk you can sweetheart." I look at her a bit shook. "I know you're big, but I don't mind you nursing. It doesn't make a difference whether you nurse while you're big or small, it's all your milk either way sweet girl."

I pause for a bit unsure but mommy takes out one of her breasts cupping it. I slowly move closer to her going to latch. "Good girl" she says. It feels like the first time I had her milk all over again. My cheeks feel quite warm but it doesn't bother me too much as I continue nursing.

I really don't know how anyone could love me so much, but my mommy does and that makes me the happiest girl alive. I still don't believe she's just mine, my mommy. I look up at her so content, seeing the love her eyes hold for me.

Twenty

I wake up to full darkness, it's probably still very late in the night. I'm feeling very hot and I realise it's because I'm sleeping in an awkward position on top of mommy. I shift over, pulling the blankets off me, pushing them to mommy's side. My breathing feels very unusual, my nose is a bit blocked but It isn't too much of a big deal.

I decide to get a bit of water from downstairs and maybe a snack. When I open the door I'm met with complete darkness, I look for the light switches but I can't find them so I decide to 'abort mission'. I could wake mommy up but that wouldn't be very nice. I climb back onto the bed and stare at the ceiling, shuffling around a few times.

Mommy stretches her arm out searching for something. That's until she puts her hand on me and suddenly pulls me right next to her. I groan a bit but sleeping cuddled up right against her feels really good so I let it be. Eventually my eyes feel heavy so I close them falling asleep at some point.

The second time I wake up, I feel absolutely horrible. My ears feel clogged, my throat feels dry, I'm feeling cold but mommy says I'm quite warm, everything hurts! Only one nostril works and it makes a squeaky noise every time I breathe in it's so annoying. It's only the morning and I'm already done for the day.

"Mommy no! Icky!" I say pushing her hand away.

"I know you feel icky sweet girl but you need to eat so mommy can give you something to make you feel better." I turn on my belly not interested in what mommy's telling me right now. "Can you have one pancake for mommy? Just one."

"Yucky pancake." I say tucking my head under the pillow. Mommy grabs the pillow off me and picks me up sitting me on her lap. I whine wanting to lay back in bed. I look at mommy who seems to be already dressed for work, she's definitely going to have to leave me behind today. I'm not going to school feeling like this, that's final whether she likes it or not!

"The pancakes weren't yucky when you had them yesterday" she says raising an eyebrow "What would you like then? You have to pick something to eat mama." Mommy says. I attempt to get off her lap but mommy pulls me right back. I try to fight her some more but she's extra strong so I eventually give up.

Mommy lets out a sigh starring right into my soul. She then unbuttons her shirt and lifts up her bra. She changes my position on her lap, now cradling me. Mommy holds her nipple between her pointer and middle finger guiding it towards my mouth. "Can you have milky then?" I quickly nod grinning pretty wide, mommy chuckles shaking her head. I really don't want food but mommy's milky I can have any day. "Good girl" mommy says when I latch on. I look up at mommy enjoying the moment. I like spending time with mommy. Even when she threatens to punish me, I still love her a lot.

I've realised that making mommy angry is currently my favourite thing to do, mostly because she usually doesn't carry out the punishment so it's nice being naughty. I have her wrapped around my pinky! She doesn't need to know that though. "What are you smiling at?" Mommy asks. I shake my head receiving a glare of suspicion.

Mommy suddenly takes her boobie out of my mouth, quickly changing my position and puts her other boobie in my mouth. It all happens so quickly I don't even get the opportunity to complain. I look at mommy's other nipple and poke it and twist it around curiously. Mommy doesn't say anything so I assume she doesn't mind the poking. My belly feels really full now, but I still want my milky.

"Nollani!!" Mommy shrieks startling me pulling her boobie from my mouth. "We don't bite, that hurt mommy." She scolds. I feel tears in my eyes, holding back from crying. I bury my face in mommy's chest. "Bubs I know you're upset but we don't bite! If you would like to bite something you tell mommy then we can figure something out. Not mommy's nipple." I don't respond, keep my face in between her boobies. I don't want them anymore anyway.

Mommy pats my bottom causing a thudding sound. "Mommy! Stop!" I squirm trying to move my butt away from her hand.

"I think someone needs their bum changed!" Mommy whispers into my hear. I'm about to protest but let out a squeak instead when mommy puts a finger in my diaper. "Very full!" Mommy says more to herself. I stick my fingers in my mouth not wanting to respond to anything. Mommy stands up leaving me lying on her bed. "I'll be right back don't move." I think this is my opportunity to hide but I want my bum changed. I giggle at the way that sounds.

Mommy comes back with another diaper, wipes and some stupid cream. I turn on my belly crawling away quickly but mommy grabs my ankle and brings me back to the position she left me in. "No want diapey mommy! No want!" I say kicking.

"Okay, okay! What if we try a pull up instead?" I'm not too sure what that is but I nod watching mommy leave again and coming back a few seconds later. It's another diaper but this some looks almost like big girl undies. Mommy works quickly changing me, putting the big-girl-undies-diapey on. It feels way lighter and way more comfortable.

"Why no put Lani in undies-diapey first!" I ask pouting with my arms folded. Mommy doesn't respond but instead takes my binky, quickly stuffing it in my mouth. Stupid mommy! She takes my nightie off and replaces it with a weird shirt that goes all the way and buttons up in between my legs. She wraps a blanket around me and gives me a dozen of kisses, chuckling softly at my fake frustration.

Mommy then picks me up taking me all the way downstairs. "Tinkerbell?" She asks. I wiggle my bottom happily in her arms. "Pancake?" She asks, making me suckle quickly on my binky hiding my head in her neck. "Alright then mommy's going to eat allllll alone." She tells me looking really sad and that make me very sad.

"Otay! I have one pancake, no more!" I manage to say with my binky in my mouth. Mommy smiles kissing my forehead. "Tinkerbell?" I ask again wanting to know if the deal still stands.

"We can watch it while mommy feeds you lovebug." I nod laying down on mommy's shoulder watching her every move.

"Mommy no go to work ?"

"No sweet-thing, not with my baby feeling icky, I'll have Tisha in charge today while mommy takes care of you." I smile behind my binky feeling very fuzzy. That's until she wipes my nose leaving me in a sore-mood. What a party pooper!

Twenty one

"Lani, where are mommy's glasses?" Mommy asks looking in her office drawers. She sits down having given up searching and looks at me. I wonder if she can see me. "Nollani?"

"What glasses? I don't know what you're talking about." I say pretending to straighten out my dress so I don't have to look up at her. Mommy and I had a really fun day today. She allowed me to skip another day of school because I hadn't completed recovery from my flu. The best part was that I could cling to her all I want just because I'm sick. I think mommy also just wanted another day off today, the poor old woman.

Mommy ruined the fun when she told me she has a stupid work event tonight which she has to attend and she's planning on taking me to Aunty Ela and Lana's. I hardly even know them. Mommy thinks it's going to be very fun because I have their little - Rylie - to play with. My best decision was to hide her glasses because I know she doesn't drive without her glasses. I mean why is she even wearing glasses to a fancy event?

"You better not lie to me! Get my glasses before I count to three." I look at mommy seeing a her giving me the mommy look. I wanna lie and say I don't know where they are but I don't want to get in more trouble. I also don't want to admit I hid her glasses because I'm going to get in trouble as well. "One, you better start moving your little butt." I hold my hands behind my back swinging from side to side nervously. "Two! Young lady you better not test me." Mommy says now very upset. I turn around quickly going to get the glasses where I hid them.

I get to mommy's room opening her underwear drawer, taking her glasses and heading back to her office. Her glasses were right under her nose she could've found them herself. Mommy stretches out her hand, waiting for me to place the glasses in hand. I walk closer to her handing her the glasses. She swats my bum making me squeal. I cover my bottom looking at her with a pout, just to be dramatic. "No hiding mommy's glasses, that's getting added to your rules." Mommy says wiping her glasses and putting them on carefully so she doesn't mess her up makeup. I should've locked her car keys inside her car instead, just kidding!

I mean she looks really beautiful in emerald green dress it goes really well with her complexion and dark hair. Not going to the event would be a waste BUT I don't like the fact that she's abandoning me. "Mommy don't go! Pleeease." I sit on her lap and put my head on her chest.

"Bubs, mommy has to be there." She says kissing my forehead. "How about mommy gives you one of her shirts so it feels like mommy's around?" I nod after thinking about it.

"How about I go to Aunty Jas' house instead?" I ask deciding that spending time there would be better than with Ela and her crew. Mommy furrows her eyebrows before answering me.

"So now you don't mind regressing in front of Hafsa?" I throw my head backwards because mommy's making this conversation difficult for me. Apparently, Aunty Jas has known about my age regression for quite some time now. She knew this because mommy's a caregiver and saw signs in me that almost resembled mommy's previous little. Apparently that's also the reason why when Hafsa and I decided to drink, Aunty Jasmine called mommy to sell me out to my "mommy".

"I won't be little mommy!"

"No, you're going to Lana's plus Jasmine lives a bit far, half an hour away is pretty far. It didn't end well the last time you went there." Mommy winks at me with a playful grin. I feel my cheeks tingling from the memory. She always brings up the incident and teases me about it.

"No teasing mommy!" I say hiding my face. "Fine! I'll go to Aunty Ela's" I say.

Mommy swiftly stands up still holding me. She grabs a bag with items she thinks I might need including her shirt and then she takes her purse. The drive there is the worst, it just felt very quick. Mommy tried to tell me how excited Rylie is to finally meet me, but I don't want to even listen.

"Ready?" Mommy asks opening my door handing me her 'comfort shirt'. I huff pouting at her, what kind of question is that. I'm never talking to her for the rest of my life. She places her hand on my cheek and rubs it with her thumb, I lean into her touch not wanting her to stop. She picks me up, grabbing my bag and walks up to the front door. Mommy doesn't even ring the door bell because a girl runs out to hug my mommy screaming "Aunty Naina!"

Aunty Ela and Lana stand by the door watching us. Aunty Lana eventually walks up to mommy cooing at me. I turn away from her lying my head on mommy's shoulder. "Uh-uh-uh cupcake, you can't hide from me." and I cling to mommy like I've never before.

"Mama she not want you?" I hear the girl AKA Rylie saying to Aunty Lana.

"No baby." I feel tears sting my eyes, mommy rubs my back gently shushing me when she hears me start sniffling.

"Hey sweetie, there's no need to cry. We're going to have so much fun, unlike your boring mommy." Aunty Ela comes over and says. Aunty Lana slaps her arm telling her to read the room.

"Mommy's gonna be back very soon pumpkin I promise" Mommy says kissing me and whispering sweet words in my ear. I'm abruptly taken out of her arms. I wail kicking around trying to reach out to mommy but she walks away not even looking back at me. I scream bloody murder when I'm taken inside. I eventually notice Aunty Lana's the one holding me. She sits down with me in her lap slowly rocking me. I try to pull back but she holds me tightly against her chest, rubbing my back.

It takes me a while to calm down but when I do I notice Rylie sitting next to us. I also notice she's been the one gently rubbing my back. She smiles at me and I smile back even though my heart is pretty broken. She looks really kind and her hair looks really cool. It's short like her mommy's but she has blue dyed ends.

"All better?" Aunty Lana asks looking at me. I shake my head. "Why not cupcake?" I shrug not wanting to speak, where did mommy put my binky anyway.

"Binky p'ease." I say to Aunty Lana who looks at her wife a bit confused.

"She want her paci mama duhh!" Rylie says pulling a funny face to her mama making me giggle. I like her a lot already.

"Hey that's no way to speak to your mama you little squid!" Aunty Ela says and receives an eye roll From Rylie. Aunty Ela goes to tickle Rylie and I look at them amused not noticing that Aunty Lana had stood up with me on her hip. She clips my binky on the top of my dress, the clip wasn't there before, but I brush it off taking my paci and suckling on it. After a while of sitting on Aunty Lana's lap I feel a tap on my leg.

"Nola? Wanna play wiff my toys? They're really fun." I nod taking her word for it wiggling down. I focus on the nickname she used, my mother used to call me that so it's very special. She grabs my hand taking me but more like dragging me to her playroom. Silly girl.

Twenty Two

Rylie's playroom is really messy. Mommy would explode if my playroom looked like hers. I think it means her mommies are way more fun compared to my mommy who wants everything clean.

"What you wanna play first Nola?" I look around and my eyes land on an ice cream shop toy set. I point showing her my choice. "Ice cream shop! Mama and mommy are always bad customers." She says and we hear soft chuckles. Rylie dramatically marches over shooing her mommies away. When she comes back she offers to play the customer so I'm the shopkeeper.

We start playing and she's so funny. I'm laughing so much, I lost my binky somewhere during the game but luckily it's still clipped on my dress. She's ordering all the yucky flavours. "Strawberry, chocolate and grape ice cream please."

"That yucky! But sorry, ice cream machine broken no more ice cream." I say.

"Hey! I'm a plumber I fix it." she says in a silly voice pulling her hair under nose like a moustache. I giggle face palming, I don't think plumbers fix ice cream machines but I move over anyway letting her do her thing.

"P'ease be gentle with my ice cream machine Mr plumber!" I tell her sternly trying to play along.

"I got it!" She says. I look at her curiously watching her fiddling around. "Looks like the machine is clogged! Let me get my tools." I watch her scrambling around grabbing random toys to use as tools. "Looks like I forgot to bring my ice cream machine tools...I'll just have to use the ones for the toilet." She says giggling.

"No! That yucky!" I yell giggling as well. She goes on working on the machine with me still watching her. When she's done we go back to playing customer and shopkeeper. Aunty Lana walks in and comes over to me putting her hand on my back. She leans over whispering in my ear.

"Can Aunty Lana take you to the potty baby? It's going to be really quick then you can come back and play." She says stretching her hand out for me to hold. I don't need to use the potty right now but I can still try going. I still have on my big girl panties so I don't want to have an accident.

"Otay." I say holding her hand. She takes Rylie's hand too, who puffs out annoyed with her Mama.

Rylie goes off to potty in her bathroom while I go on with Aunty Lana to a different bathroom. "Do you need me to help you baby?" I shake my head 'no'. "Do you want me to leave you or stand here and wait for you?" She asks.

"Wait p'ease." I respond. She nods closing the door slightly. I lift up my dress pulling my panties down and sit on the toilet waiting to go. Once I'm done I roll some tissue wiping and fixing my clothes. "Help wash my hands?" I ask Aunty Lana opening the door.

"Sure cupcake." She picks me up sitting me on the basin counter. She rolls up the sleeves of the shirt I'm wearing under my dress and puts two pumps of soap in my hands. I wash my hands under the water but I still want to play with the water when she closes the tap.

"Hands still yucky Aunty Lana!" I tell her whining.

"Uh-uh, they seem clean to me." She says taking me off the counter. I fold my arms walking ahead of her. We get back to the play room and Rylie's playing with one of her dolls. Aunty Lana leaves us in the playroom again but I'm obviously still upset.

"Wanna play wiff my doll?" She asks looking concerned. I shake my head pouting. "What happen?" She asks.

"Aunty Lana no let me wash my hands." I say. I see Rylie's in deep thought before she smiles at me mischievously.

"Secret mission, us go to my bathroom and wash your hands?" I smile liking the sound of that. Rylie goes first tiptoeing and I follow her putting my hand over my mouth so I don't giggle. We get to her bathroom and do a little happy dance.

Rylie lets me stand on her step stool while she climbs up on the counter. She opens the tap letting me wash my hands and she joins me. We eventually end up splashing each other and our clothes end up really wet. My belly hurts from all the giggling but it does a huge flip when the door opens revealing a very upset Aunty Ela.

"Ry-ry? What are you two doing?" She asks whispering. "You guys are soaking wet, let's get you two changed before your mama sees you." I thought Aunty Ela was supposed to be the strict one, I mean she looks the part.

"Babe is everything okay?" I hear Aunty Lana yell from the kitchen.

"Yeah, we're fine." She's lying, she's a naughty mommy. Aunty Ela changes us and takes us to watch something. "Lani do you want your babba love?" She asks and I nod quickly smiling at her. Aunty Lana comes out with my babba sitting right next to me. I'm taken aback when she pulls me onto her lap and positions me so that I'm sitting comfortably. She brings my babba to my mouth and I have my milky content.

I rather have milky from mommy but this will do. I have my babba whilst also trying to focus on what's playing on the TV. Rylie seems to be enjoying it so I try to follow along. I eventually fall asleep against Aunty Lana's chest. I only wake up when I feel something soft being placed under my butt. I whine not happy about being woken up but fall back to sleep after I'm handed mommy's shirt and picked up again.

"Hi, pumpkin." I hear mommy coo and open my eyes slowly. I reach out towards mommy whining softly. She unbuckles me from my booster seat and holds me tightly against her. I snuggle into her realising how much I missed her. "Did you have fun tonight?" I nod closing my eyes again. "Aunty Ela and Lana said you were a really good girl tonight. Mommy's very proud of you sweet girl." Mommy says giving me a few kisses.

Mommy takes us inside and lays me on her bed resting right next to me. She goes away making me cry softly. "Mommy, right here sweetheart." she comes back wearing her nighty, slipping my binky in my mouth. She comforts me patting my bottom and stroking my cheek, putting me to sleep once again.

Twenty Three

I'm currently sitting outside my grandmother's house waiting for mommy to come get me. Nothing eventful really happened, besides how my dad insisted on taking me to class this morning. I didn't wanna tell him someone else was gonna do it because he would've asked me a whole lot of nonsense so I gave in. When he dropped me off he said to call him when I was ready for him to come pick me up, it was weird but I still agreed. Mommy was a bit worried when I told her about the change of plans but I managed to convince her.

When I see Mommy's car pull up I quickly gather my things and walk really fast towards the car. Mommy gets out and I drop everything running to her. "Oh hi pumpkin." Mommy says catching me in her arms. I cling to her taking in her warmth, her scent, her love, everything. I told my grandmother about mommy, I just lied and said she's my new landlady.

"I missed you!" I say burying my head in her neck.

"Mommy missed you too sweet-thing" she says and sets me down making me whine in displeasure. "Can I get a kiss?" She asks pouting expectantly. I peck her lips quickly after looking around, making sure no one is looking. I get my things and throw them in the car. Mommy opens my door for me to get in but that's not happening today. I run right around going to the passenger door, by the time mommy realises what's going on it's too late because I'm already inside, shutting the door on her.

"Too slow!" I say giggling. It backfires though because the door is swiftly opened and she carries me over her shoulder to my booster seat quickly buckling me in.

"Too slow!" She says, making me pout turning away from her. She gets in the car and drives us home, not moved by little tantrum. "Baby can you open the box right next to you? There's something I need you to hand me that's inside the box." I wasn't gonna listen to her but what she's talking about sounds important so I get the box opening it. It's full of crumbled paper making me wonder what it is she might want in here.

"See it?" I furrow my eyebrows moving the paper away. My eyes go really wide when I see a pair of sparkling tinkerbell shoes, they even have the white fluffy ball ontop. I take one shoe handing it over to mommy. "They're yours silly! I was just fooling with you." Mommy says chuckling.

"Really?" I ask already taking off my shoes to put on my tinker shoes. This is probably the best gift I've ever gotten. Aunty Jasmine used to buy me loads of precious gifts but this one it precious-er. I feel my eyes tearing up. "Thank you mommy!" I manage to say with a lump in my throat.

"Aww you're very welcome pumpkin."

When we arrive home I quickly unbuckle my seat belt ready to give my shoes a trial run, literally. I open my door shooting across the front yard giggling. I run around before noticing that there's an open gate covered in vines. I look back at mommy, who looks back at me suspiciously. I run straight for the gate and surprisingly she doesn't stop me. When I get to the other side I notice there's a sandpit with monkey bars over it, a swing set and a slide. Ahead is a short fence around a pool, that looks very well kept but mommy never comes here.

I look back seeing mommy standing smiling back at me. The play area doesn't look new, one of the buckets still has sand in them, meaning that someone used it not too long ago. "Never showed me backyard!" I look at mommy a bit disappointed.

"When I wanted to show you around the house the day you moved in you didn't want to leave the playroom baby. That's why I've never brought you here." I nod remembering how I told mommy to take the house tour alone. Mommy walks up to me squatting next to me

"Other little?" I ask and mommy pushes my hair behind my ear.

"Yes love, she used to play in the sandpit mostly, the other things were too big for her." I nod once again.

"Me allowed to play here?"

"Yes you are baby, all yours now!" Mommy says.

"Swim?"

"Can you?" I quickly shake my head. I was never taught how to swim, I usually watched people swim. The few times I've been asked if I could I usually lied, until the day my lie backfired but that's a story for another day.

"I play now mommy?" I jump excitedly.

"Go ahead, mommy going inside but I'll come out through that door." She says pointing to the sliding door that leads out here. I've never seen this door from inside. I think i need to explore the house once I'm done playing out here.

"Otay" I respond running to climb up the monkey bars. Mommy suddenly closes the gate locking it but I shrug it off continuing to play. It's not too long after mommy opens the door.

"Do you need to potty baby?" Mommy yells making me blush at the thought of the neighbours hearing her.

"Mommy Nooo! No need to potty!" I yell stomping my foot. Mommy nods going away but still leaving the door open. Eventually I'm covered in sand everywhere. I take off my tinker shoes because I need to keep them clean, afterwards I pull down my shorts dusting them off and throwing them aside then it's my shirt. I look at the pool realising it would help wash the sand way, It doesn't even look that deep. I walk around looking for the gate then I finally find it, wiggling happily.

"You're going to get yourself a sore little bottom Nollani." Mommy says warningly startling me. I quickly walk around going to the swings, pretending I wasn't about to open the gate to the pool. "what happened to your clothes young lady?" I point climbing on the swing. "Words! I can't hear pointing." Mommy says in her mommy voice which scares me a bit.

"Clothes over there mommy!" I say and she goes over to pick them up.

"No going near the pool, you have about...10 minutes more to play then it's bath time, okay?" Mommy says looking at me.

I nod but quickly say "yes Mommy" when she lifts an eyebrow, she's so scary sometimes.

"Come mama, bathtime." Mommy says, there's no way, it's only been 10 seconds.

"No mommy too early. I still playing." Mommy comes over but I run away, I though I was really fast but mommy catches me in a slit second, I kick around trying to get down but mommy slaps my butt making me stop. I hide my face on her shoulder upset with her.

"You can play tomorrow lovebug. Mommy has to get you clean for dinner time right now." She tells me but I'm still not convinced. "Then you can have mommy's milky" mommy says in my ear making me shoot up and look at her boobies.

"Silly girl" Mommy chuckles setting me on my feet. I run to the bathroom having completely forgotten I was upset a second ago.

Twenty Four

Hanaina's Pov

"Mommy bath bomb!" I nod to acknowledge her request.

"Just a second baby, let mommy get your towel." I run out to get her towel, knowing the mischief this little one can get to in seconds. I come back grabbing a tray of bath bombs "Okay which one? Fairy dust, unicorns sparkles or strawberry shortcake?"

"Mmm...unico'n spa'kles!" I smile amused by her pronunciation.

"Good choice." I say dropping the bathbomb in the water before getting her undressed. "Ready to get in?" I get a nod. "1, 2, 3, jump!" I put her in the tub splashing water everywhere.

"Mommy, Rylie and me play with water and get all wet."

"Really? That's why your clothes were wet when I took them out of your bag." I say

"Mhm, but Rylie's mommy say not tell Aunty Lana. Her a naughty mommy!" Nollani says with the most adorable expression on her face.

"She is isn't she!" I say mimicking her expression laughing at her silliness.

She takes her washcloth deciding she wants to give herself a bath. She gets distracted by her toys so I give her a quick bath before she notices she's not doing it herself anymore. I wash her hair and there's grains of sand everywhere. I've moved on but it brings back the memories I had with my previous little girl, how she'd come back from playing outside covered in sand. Now I regret getting that sandpit because it's way too messy.

I let Nollani play for a bit longer otherwise we're going to end up fighting to get her out the tub. "All done?" I ask once I'm satisfied with how long she's been playing. I don't think I've met a child that loves playing like Nollani does, but I'd rather have her playing than creating trouble.

"Nooo!" She says smiling at me cheekily.

"Uh-uh-uh, out you go." I say holding the towel out to wrap her in.

"Mommy- "

"No excuses! Mommy doesn't want a sick baby again." I pull the plug letting the water drain.

"Me big girl!" She corrects me huffing.

"Of course you are pumpkin. Now come." I sit on the edge of the bathtub with the towel laid on top of me. I pick her up sitting her on my lap, with her leaning against me. She's sulking while I wipe her but I'm not letting her get her way, not today at least. "Look at all that sand." I say pointing at the empty bathtub.

Nollani doesn't respond but turns around putting her face against my breasts. It's only then that I realise how full they are, I have to get some milk in this girls belly or I'm gonna be the one sulking. I stand up going into her room and settle on the rocking chair. She looks up at me confused until she sees me lifting up my shirt.

"Milky now?" She asks with her eyes curiously wide.

"Yes love, mommy's really hurting, you need to have a little bit of milky then you can have proper food." I say poking her stomach making her giggle. I help her latch on sighing at the relief I feel. My other breast is leaking so I use the towel between us to help catch the milk until I switch sides.

She's playing around on my lap, something she does very often when I'm feeding her. I scratch her back to stop her fidgeting because she ends up pulling on my nipple which really hurts. I instantly feel her relax but my worry now is her having an accident on my lap.

When my breast is almost empty I quickly change her position to latch on my other breast. Nollani eagerly grabs my breast to latch on but it doesn't go well because the milk gets sprayed all over the her. I chuckle softly but little miss is not impressed. I see her pouting about to cry, so I bounce my leg wiping the milk off her face and get her latched on again. "There you go sweetheart, you're fine." I say softly, patting her bottom.

She's looking up into my eyes now but I can tell with each blink that she's getting sleepy. I remove my breast from her mouth working quickly to replace it with her pacifier. She babbles at me angry and it takes me by surprise. "Ohh such a little girl." I say gently kissing her forehead. I've lost my experience with an infant but it shouldn't be that difficult.

I lay Nollani on her changing mat and she flips around quickly about to crawl away. I quickly grab her ankle holding her so she doesn't fall off. "Naughty!" I scold making her cry. I take the opportunity to quickly get her dressed and pick her up once I'm done to calm her down. "Okay, okay, mommy's sorry baby. You're such a good girl, aren't you?" I say giving her random kisses between my words. I put her paci back in her mouth receiving loud suckling noises.

I rub her back, going downstairs to get us something to eat. I plate up on one plate deciding to let her eat with me because she's already had milk. I alternate between the two of us, feeding her then myself. Just like I had assumed Nollani is full much quicker. She's now trying to grab the plate and flip it over.

"No lovebug." I tell her placing her on the floor to crawl so I can finish up. When I'm done, I take her upstairs to put her to bed but she's still playing around, obviously not ready to sleep. I let her play until I see her getting tired. I sit her on my lap bouncing her in a rhythmic pattern, simultaneously patting her diapered bottom. Once she's asleep I lay her on the bed placing pillows around her so she doesn't fall during her sleep.

I get up to take a quick shower so I can get some rest. Tomorrow's Saturday but I need to go to the office to finish up on something. I can't help but dread having to wake Nollani up in the morning to take her with, but I'll deal with that when the time comes. I tuck myself right beside my baby kissing her forehead and getting some shut eye.

Twenty Five

"Baby! You need to come down, time is not on our side."

"Just a minute!"

Yeah, that was a lie. I'm nowhere near going downstairs. I concluded that if she can deprive me of my sleep I can delay her morning by just a few minutes. I mean I'm dressed and ready but I need a little more time in bed. This is my opportunity to catch up on last night's dream. I climb on my bed and go under the covers. I decide the best thing to do is to disguise myself by neatly putting the covers over me and hide my head under the pillows.

"Nollani?" I hear mommy call me, I respond so she doesn't get suspicious.

"Coming!" I yell back. I hear her heels on the floor, which lets me know she's coming up the stairs. I lay completely still hoping she won't find me and she'll leave to go to the office alone. Her steps stop somewhere near my door before she walks away. I lift my head up to see if I'm still safe and I'm met with a very stern mommy looking right back at me. She's leaning on the door frame with her arms folded. I swear I heard her walking away, she fooled me.

"I'm going to start counting till three and if you're not out of that bed with your shoes on you're going to be very unhappy." I don't even wait for her to start counting. I jump out of bed picking my shoes up and running down the stairs. "No running!" She says so I slow down. I really thought I hid myself well, how on earth did she see me? She's definitely a psychic of some sorts. When I get to the bottom of the stairs I realise I forgot my backpack in my room. I hop anxiously biting my finger trying to figure out what to do.

"Fuck it, I can survive without a bag." I say.

"That's strike number 2, young lady!" She says patting my bottom firmly. I'm startled because she keeps appearing everywhere randomly. "Go get that bag quickly." I go up to my room and notice my bed is neatly made again. I grab my backpack quickly going downstairs. I close the door behind me and get into the car sitting in my booster seat. It's a bit embarrassing to sit on it while I'm big but it's just mommy and I in the car, it isn't a big deal.

My stomach rumbles and mommy looks at me through the rear view mirror. "Your stomach is pretty angry isn't it?" She says cooing at me. "I'll get you something to eat in a bit lovebug."

"With coffee? Pleaaaaaase, just for today!" I say trying to sound as convincing as possible.

"You can have just a little bit of my coffee, you're not getting your own."

"Mommy!" I whine.

"That or nothing."

"Fine!" I say Kicking her seat a few times.

"You're behaving worse than your little self right now, what's going on?" I don't know why I'm being so cranky this morning but being woken up early has something to do with it. "Do you need me to hold you?" Mommy asks making my cheeks warm. I shrug not knowing how to respond to that.

I end up feeling guilty and remain quiet throughout the remainder of the car ride. When mommy hands me a my breakfast wrap and juice I take it without complaining. She gave me a bit of her coffee and I took it happily. I sort of felt bad for behaving so bad when all she ever does is love me. Mommy opens the door for me once she's parked, because it has the childlock on. I jump to hug her and I can tell she's surprised.

"What is it love?" She asks picking me up. Right now I really don't care who sees us I just wanna make it up to my mommy.

"I'm sorry for acting naughty this morning. I'll do better, I promise." I say giving her a kiss on the forehead.

"Well thank you for the apology, I think mommy should've told you that we were going to come here today. I forgive you but I'm still holding the 2 strikes." She says making me whine.

"What about now?" I ask giving her a kiss.

"You can't bribe me with kisses baby." She laughs setting me down.

"That's not fair, you do it to me all the time." I say helping her get some of her files from the car.

"Well aren't you so gullible." I groan following her once she locks the car. Mommy puts on her boss face, occasionally responding to her employees when they greet her. We get to her office floor and I dump my stuff running off to go find Latisha.

"Hiiii!" I yell throwing her door open.

"Ohhh! Mommy's girl!" I roll my eyes annoyed. "Let's go to your mommy before she calls me in." Tisha says getting up from her desk. I follow her, going back to mommy's office. When I walk in mommy points at my bag that I dumped on the floor. I pick it up putting it on the couch and let Tisha and mommy talk. When Tisha's about to leave I walk quickly to follow her.

"No! Latisha has a lot to do you need to let her work." I open my mouth to argue but mommy doesn't let me. "You promised to behave better!" I want to explode in frustration. I go over to the couch throwing myself on it and turn my back towards mommy. I sit for quite sometime before I'm picked up. I don't have the energy to fight her so I let her hold me.

"Come here sweetheart." Mommy says. She sits down on the couch with me now on her lap. She holds me against her chest and I use it as an opportunity to ask for milk indirectly. I latch onto her boobie over her clothes and mommy reacts quickly by pulling me away. "You're going to get my dress wet!" She says while pulling her dress down to reveal her bra. I latch on suckling eagerly and surpassingly mommy doesn't tell me to slow down.

I unlatch trying to catch my breath but mommy mistakes it as I'm done and puts her boobie back away. "Mommy no!" I say taking out her other boobie and having my milky again. Tisha walks in making me squeak. I cover my face because that way she can't see me anymore. Mommy and Tisha go on as if nothing's wrong. I peak looking up at Latisha and she winks at me making me hide again.

"Why are you flushed." Mommy asks once Tisha leaves. I look at mommy sternly because it's her fault that Latisha knows mommy breastfeeds me. "What?" Mommy asks when she notices me glaring at her.

"Tisha see me! You give me milky! Mommy fault." I say making sure to quickly latch back on before mommy thinks I'm done again.

"You could've told mommy you don't want milk!" Mommy says. "You also could've stopped having milk when Latisha walked in but you carried on suckling." Groan at mommy's response. I mean she has a point but it's still her fault. It's her boobies, it's just unfortunate that they have my milky. I rub my teeth together on her nipple, not too hard because I'm not trying to get in too much trouble.

"I dare you!" Mommy says with a lifted eyebrow. I let go of her nipple getting off her lap. I grab my bag taking out my binky and colouring book. I lay on my belly and go on with my colouring and Mommy goes back to her boring work. I eventually get bored and sneak out crawling out of her office. I get up running to Tisha's office. She isn't there so I figured she's probably in Lydia's office so I walk all the way to that department and I find twittle dee and twittle dumb cackling together. I hide my binky in my pocket because Lydia's going to tease me if she sees it.

I don't know what told me to look behind me but when I do I see mommy walking in my direction. She doesn't see me luckily so I quickly hide behind one of the bookshelves. Mommy walks right by me mumbling. She looks very upset, Tisha is in so much trouble I giggle excitedly. Mommy turns around looking right at me. She comes over picking me up and the smile on my face vanishes.

She enters Lydia's office and the room goes silent. Tisha jumps off the table she was sitting on. "Ms Zalda? I was..."

"Get to my office!" Mommy say standing by the door. Tisha quickly walks by and mommy lands a smacks on her bottom. Tisha jumps up making me laugh hysterically. Mommy glares at me, and I shove my face in her neck. We walk back to mommy's office and mommy still looks upset.

"Latisha, get your work from your office, you'll be doing it right next to me. Hopefully that will keep you from running off to other departments when we have something important to finish today." Mommy tells Tisha in her mommy voice. I'm still pretty amused by the whole situation. I can't believe mommy spanked Tisha.

"Yes Ms Zalda." Tisha says responds leaving to get her stuff.

Mommy puts me down and bends over to meet me at eye level. "You do not sneak away from me. Mommy got very worried when she didn't find you in Latisha's office or anywhere nearby." I look at my feet and mommy uses her finger to lift my chin up. "You're going to timeout for 5 minutes."

"But mommy!" I whine. Mommy lifts her eyebrow and I know not to challenge her. I stand in the corner. Tisha comes back sitting right next to mommy and does her work. I hear them mumbling, when I look back I see mommy rubbing Tisha's back with a smile on her face. Tisha looks a bit flushed, I wonder what mommy said to her. "Mommy?"

"Huh?" Mommy responds.

"5 minutes over now." I say figuring I've been standing here for way too long.

"I don't think so, it's only been 3 minutes ." I whine leaning on the wall.

"I thirsty mommy!"

"Less than two minutes left baby!"

"I want to...to...potty!" I say after thinking for a while. Mommy chuckles calling me over to her. I climb up her lap and mommy pushes my bum to help me up. "I sowwy mommy!" I say leaning on her chest, mommy rubs me comforting me.

"Apology accepted , no more sneaking away?" I nod quickly "Can I get a kiss?" Mommy asks.

"No! Icky cooties!" Mommy laughs showering me with kisses and I melt into a pool of giggles.

"Do you wanna watch something while Mommy and Tisha work?" That sounds good to me.

"Yes p'ease!"

Twenty Six

Latisha's Pov

Weird is the best word to use to describe this situation. I mean I'm not jealous of Nollani, in fact I absolutely adore her but it was 3 years ago that I decided I didn't want Hanaina as my mama anymore. I miss her at times but being little is not something I needed anymore, I feel like the void I had before I met her was no longer there so it was an easy decision. I'm in a different stage of my life. I'm in a different relationship now, absolutely smitten in fact.

I recall how ma- Hanaina would keep me so close to her and make me feel so loved and cared for. It was me who got to sit on her lap, got to nurse, called different sweet names, had all her attention on me the list goes on. I've moved on just like she's obviously moved on. There are still some instances where I feel like she treats me like I'm a regressor which I'm not. I still love her and yes she still means the world to me but it's weird seeing your former caregiver with another little. Lucky for me though, because I got my job as her assistant back after our relationship.

"Did you miss me!" Nollani storms into my office, at this point it doesn't surprise me anymore. She can be so shy around some people and such a numb-numb around her mommy and I.

"No I did not." I say rolling my eyes at her. "How did your classes go? Wait, does your mommy know you're with me right now?" She nods quickly making me chuckle because it means she learnt her lesson the other day. I still think I got the worst punishment though, a swat on the butt with some of my colleagues watching...not cool, but at-least I got an apology.

"She forced me to attend classes today. She's such a-"

"Such a what?" I look at my boss who doesn't look very happy at the moment. I look between the two waiting for one of them to say something. I'm obviously amused by the little tension in the room. This girl cannot stay out of trouble for a second. I can't blame her, neither could I when I was her little but I was still a bit more behaved given my little age.

"-a beautiful woman, what did you think I was going to say mommy?" She asks turning the blame and batting her eyelashes innocently, she's so cheeky.

"You keep that behaviour up and you won't be coming over to Latisha." The amount of groans and whines that follow after that are just nonsensical, coming from such a little body. I'm flattered that I mean that much to her.

"So dramatic." I say under my breath and I receive a kick on my foot. Hana comes over to my side placing her hand on the table and hunches over my shoulder. She does this very often not just with me, it's almost like her way of asserting dominance. It's something Lydia fantasies about but her imagination of it is horrific. Hanaina does it absentmindedly but that's not how Lydia sees it. I roll my eyes at the thought.

"Are you rolling your eyes at me while I'm talking to you?" She asks looking at me over her glasses. I didn't realise I had actually rolled my eyes, neither did I realise she was talking, Lydia still manages to get me in trouble even when she's not around.

"N-no, sorry Miss Zalda, I wasn't paying attention." I say receiving a little snicker from Nollani. I can just tell my cheeks are pretty flushed, Hanaina makes me pretty nervous sometimes. After our relationship I had gotten so comfortable being around her to the point where I was slacking, but she obviously worked really hard to remind me of her position.

"Hmm." She hums. "I said, I need the file with all the business accounts we made with R&Jays..." She goes on to give me a few more instructions before she stands upright again. "Will it be sorted before I leave?"

"Yes ma'am" I say sounding too enthusiastic.

"You're such a star." She says looking much more relieved than when she walked in. "Don't disappoint me." She says while walking out.

"You scared of my mommy?" Nollani asks climbing onto my lap. Maybe just a little, well when she's upset then yes. I think she's such a softy but people who don't know her very well wouldn't tell. I get away with a lot of things around here, besides the time I double booked one of her meetings. Never making that mistake again. Even thinking about it is so humiliating.

"No I'm not. I just respect her a lot." She shrugs not convinced. "Let's go."

"Where? I get ice lolly?" She asks. I don't think I could ever say no to her, I'd rather get in trouble.

"If you promise to be good." She wiggles happily. I pick her up setting her on my hip. I take the elevator down to on of the filling units. I set Nollani down and she runs over to one of the ladies that work here it's very rare for her to interact with people so I'm surprised. I get what I need and I go over to get her so we can leave.

"Ice lolly, Tisha."

"We're going to get it love, just a little patience." I pick her up once again because I need to move a bit quicker. When we reach our office floor I go over to the fridge getting her what she asked for. "Don't tell your mommy." I say tucking a napkin in her shirt so she doesn't get messy. I walk back into my office hoping to get this business account issue fixed.

"I go to mommy now?" She asks. Absolutely great! Just when I told her not to tell her mommy. I nod letting her leave. I lean against my door frame trying to eavesdrop.

"Hi love bug, what's behind your back?" I hear a bit of the conversation until "Latisha Renae Reed!" Ahh shit!

Twenty Seven

I was feeling very needy today. Ever since mommy and I came home I've been following her everywhere. What makes things difficult for me is that I can't regress. I could try going into my room or to my playroom to help put me into headspace but that would mean I'd be away from mommy which I don't want. Mommy thinks I'm stressed from all the assignments and semester tests I have coming up. She suggested I take an Afternoon nap just to give my brain some rest but that's not going to happen.

I'm sitting right at her feet because I want to be close to her. She's working and is hardly paying me any attention. I don't understand how she can go to work for 8 hours and still come back home and keep working. It's quite frustrating if I'm being honest but mommy still hasn't noticed how it's affecting me.

I get up to grab a pen from her table and look through her drawers to hopefully find a few sheets of papers to brainstorm some ideas for one of my major assignments. I have no luck finding paper but I do stumble across a huge scrapbook that's decorated with pink lace and white bows. In the middle of the scrapbook are two big letters "LR".

I contemplate on whether I should open it to see what's inside because there's colourful marking paper sticking out in different areas, almost like chapters of a book. I look up at mommy and she's still glued to whatever it is she's working on. I open the book and a few notes slip while I manage to catch a few. I flip the page and my stomach does a flip.

"What the hell?"

"Hey! Language!" Mommy says but she's still not looking at me. My hands are trembling, my head is spinning, I'm biting down on my teeth so hard my jaw hurts. All I'm seeing is Latisha dressed in baby clothes some pictures have mommy in them and they both look very happy. I connect the dots in my head and I reach the conclusion that Latisha is mommy's little. That's why she forces me to go to school everyday, she doesn't give me any attention and constantly uses work as an excuse. She loves Latisha more than me.

"I'm a fucking idiot!" I yell with tears running down my face.

"Nollani!" Mommy snaps. Her expression goes from anger to shock when her eyes land on the scrapbook in my hands.

"I knew you were too good to be true. You never loved me did you?!" I say staring her dead in the eyes, shaking with anger.

"Baby-"

"Don't baby me! You don't pay attention to me anymore, you're always making excuses to go to that stupid office, you're always busy with some fucking project! You've been feeding me lies and we've been living a little lie!"

"Nollani!" She yells making me flinch. "Can I speak?"

"More lies? Sure!" I'm swiftly lifted off my feet. I start kicking and squirming in her arms. "Put me down!" I say screaming. I can't even control my cries anymore. I haven't felt hurt like this in a good while. She doesn't listen to me, instead she lets me throw my fit until I'm limp in her arms. I lay my head on her shoulder because she's been my source of comfort for the past 2 months.

"Can you listen to me now?" I don't respond because surely there's no way shes going to defend herself from this one. "Look up please." She says very calm and I do. In fact I feel so much rage that I look at her as if challenging her. She sits back down in her chair with me on her lap. I scoot off choosing to stand on my feet, than to sit on someone else's mommy.

Hanaina picks up the scrapbook placing it on the table. She turns to the very back of it and she points to a date "24/06/2014 - 17/12/2021", then she looks back up me. "That's when Latisha and I ended it." She says with her finger on the latter date. I look at her blankly, so Tisha's her notorious previous little?

She then reaches into one of the drawers and pulls out a second scrapbook. This one is decorated with pastel colours and has a big letter N on it. Mine? "Wanna look at it with me?" she asks reaching for me. I walk closer to her and she puts me on her lap. I snuggle closer into her. She opens the book and it's pictures of me, I look up at her a bit surprised and she gives me a smile in return. We go through a few of my pictures and I giggle when I see a picture of me playing in the sandpit after having abandoned my clothes. Mommy has it titled 'My Nakey Little Girl'.

Mommy closes the book and shrink into her when she looks at me. "Mommy loves you so much sweet girl. I know I've been very selfish and paying too much attention to my work but Mommy's going to work on that. You're my baby now and I promise to make it up to you." My eyes go blurry with tears, tears of guilt.

"I sorry mommy." I say plunging my face into her boobies. She rubs my back reassuring me. "No want Tisha's book here!" I say, my words muffled against her chest. I look up waiting for her to say something.

"She doesn't know I made this for her. I was planning on giving it to her soon. It's going to be gone by tomorrow though I promise." Mommy smiles softly, kissing my forehead. "Such a jealous girl." She says and I whine rubbing my face against her chest.

My head feels fuzzy, I can't even think straight. I whine feeling restless and mommy moves me making me straddle her lap. She reaches her hand into my shirt and scratches my back. It only works to calm me down for a short while before I'm back to whining again. I squirm restlessly wanting some comfort, Mommy exposes her boob. "Mi'ky!" I say as best as I could in the moment.

"I know sweetheart." She says adjusting my head. She rubs her nipple against my lips and I latch on. "That's a good girl." She says rocking us back and forth. "Such a good girl."

Twenty Eight

"Mommy no pants."

"No?"

"Uh-uh." I say dramatically folding my arms over my chest and shaking my head.

"Your shirt barely covers your bottom love, your diapey's going to be on show. How about a skirt?" Mommy asks holding it up for me to see.

"Nu-uh!"

"Can I put you in a onesie?" I quickly shake my head not budging. Mommy nods. "Then off you go." She says taping my diapered bottom making me glare at her. "No running down the stairs and be a good girl! Mommy's coming down in a second." I run off before mommy could even finish her sentence. I slow down when I reach the stairs, sitting on my bum and scoot all the way down. Mommy doesn't like me going down alone but she lets me do it all by myself sometimes if I promise to be responsible.

I hop to the kitchen deciding to get a snack to eat while I wait for mommy. The easiest thing for me to reach right now is the fridge so I place my step stool close to the fridge and pull on the handle to get an ice lolly. I get distracted and start scooping a bit of the ice on the sides of the freezer and contently eat them. Mommy says they're not safe to eat but who cares what mommy says.

"What are you doing?" Mommy says making my snap my head in her direction. She's standing with her hands on her hips. "It hasn't even been 5 minutes. And what did I say about eating that ice?" Mommy says raising an eyebrow. I shrug. Mommy comes over picking me up saying "Naughty girl!" under her breath but I hear her and I pout upset. I lay my head on her shoulder letting her do her own things.

"Would you like ham and cheese or peanut butter and Jam?" My head shoots up.

"Want all!" I yell pointing to both sandwiches. Mommy laughs putting heart shaped cut outs of bp & j sandwiches on one side of my plate and triangle cut ham sandwiches on the other side. "Apple juice please!" I add once mommy's done plating up for herself.

"Coming right up!" she says grabbing a sippy cup from the cupboard and pours some juice in my cup. It's quite impressive watching her do it all with one hand. Mommy finally sets me down letting me lead the way. "What are we watching?" She asks helping me on the couch and she sits right next to me.

I really don't care what we watch, I just want to eat my food, Mommy ends up watching her own show. Aunty Jasmine's coming over today, that's part of the reason mommy was so bothered about my diapey showing. I really don't care because what's there to hide if she already knows I'm a little.

"You need to slow down pumpkin, your food isn't going anywhere." Mommy says. I take a few gulps of my juice once I'm done with the peanut butter sandwich and move on to the ham and cheese. I don't manage to finish it so I try to feed it to mommy. "Feeding mommy soggy bread huh? so thoughtful of you baby but mommy's full." She says patting my thigh. She takes our plates to the kitchen and I follow her happily.

The doorbell goes off a while later and I run off to the door. I fiddle with it a few times and it finally clicks open when mommy does it for me. I swing the door open, running into Aunty Jasmine's arms. "Hello my angel, I'm happy to see you too." She says kissing me playfully on the crevice of my neck, making me erupt in giggles.

"Lani-" I'm startled by Hafsa jumping out from her hiding spot. When she sees me it suddenly gets very awkward, well for me because Hafsa doesn't look surprised at all. I squirm out of Aunty Jasmines arms running to hide behind mommy.

"Hey, you're okay." Mommy says reaching for me behind her legs. I feel myself slipping out of headspace. I run off to my room, mommy says something to Aunty Jasmine before she runs after me. I'm a bawling mess, what a great way for my best friend to find out about this part of my life.

Mommy picks me up holding me firmly against her chest letting me cry tucked into her. Mommy sits down with me facing her. She raises my chin forcing me to look at her once I'm calmer. "This must all be very overwhelming for you hey." I nod.

"I didn't intend for her to find out this way." I say still hiccuping.

"I know sweet-thing." She says rubbing my back. "Do you think if mommy speaks to her it'll make you feel better?" Mommy asks grabbing a wipe and wiping my face.

"She's still going to think I'm weird." I say burying my face in her breasts.

"Hafsa is a very sweet girl and I know how much she loves you, she would never think you're weird." Mommy says adjusting me on her lap. I squirm around realising I used my diaper, probably because of how anxious I got when Hafsa surprised me with her presence. When mommy notices what's happening she smiles, patting my bottom making me groan, throwing my head back. "So dramatic." She says.

She puts me on the bed and stands up grabbing a pair of underwear and shorts from my wardrobe. She undoes the tabs on my diaper and hands me a baby wipe to wipe myself down. Mommy holds my underwear out for me to step in and then my shorts. I sit on her lap once more wanting to be held a little longer. Mommy doesn't even complain about how hard I'm squishing her right now.

"Are you ready to go downstairs and talk to her?" I nod feeling a bit fidgety. "No need to be nervous my baby I'm right here." I nod taking in a deep breath. "Would it make you feel better if I told you Hafsa knows I'm a caregiver?" I look up a mommy shocked.

"She knows what that means?" Mommy nods. "Does she know..." I hesitate.

"She knows about age regressors baby, you wouldn't be the first to call me mommy in front of her." My brain is about to explode. That's why she didn't look surprised when she saw me in a diaper, and her mom casually holding me.

"What the fuck!"

"Nollani!" Mommy says stern.

"Sorry." I giggle at my slip of words. "Then do you think she knows I'm a regressor? I mean...she should. Right?" Mommy shrugs.

"There's only one way to find out." Mommy says getting up, putting me down to walk on my own. Well here goes nothing...

Twenty Nine

I try to hide behind mommy but she pushes me in front of her. Mommy sits on the couch and I lean onto her, she moves over me so I'm sitting right next to her. I look at mommy for help because I don't know how to start this conversation, Mommy gives me a nod rubbing my back.

I look in Hafsa's direction and she smiles at me. It really helps to relax my nerves a bit taking me back to how she'd give me the same smile to comfort me during my worst days. I stand up grabbing Hafsa and drag her to a different place, because I'd rather not have this conversation in front of Mommy and Aunty Jas.

The closest place is the pantry so that's where we go. I enter and Hafsa comes in closing the door behind her. It's awkwardly quiet for a few seconds before Hafsa speaks "Sooo..." she begins, unsure of what to say. "are you two like a couple-?" She asks and my eyes go wide.

"Eww no! She's just my umm..." I hesitate.

"Caregiver?" She finishes my sentence off. I nod looking down, playing with my fingers. I look up because it's really quiet and it's getting awkward.

"I'm sorry I didn't tell you." I finally say. "I didn't know how you were going to take it and I didn't want to disappoint you." I say. "BUT! You're also part of the problem because you didn't tell me you knew about these things." I say folding my arms over my chest.

"Don't even start little one." She says patting my head teasingly.

"You're so annoying!" I say shoving her off. She laughs leaning back on the door. She's staring right into my soul with a smirk.

"What ?!" I ask glancing at my outfit to spot anything weird.

"I thought you two were…fucking." She says raising her eyebrows mischievously. My cheeks start to warm up.

"You're so disgusting!" I say shoving her and she goes into a fit of laughter. I thought we were supposed to have a serious conversation, not this. Hafsa stops, frowning at me. I watch her intently wondering what she's up to now. She turns around roughly pulling the door and Mommy and Aunty Jas stumble into the room.

Mommy clears her throat straightening herself and Aunty Jas looks everywhere but at us. I giggle at how guilty they both look. "Were you not taught eavesdropping is rude!" Hafsa says folding her arms over her chest.

"Oh shush! That's rich coming from you!" Aunty Jasmine says pushing Hafsa aside. She walks over to me cupping my face. "You're so brave for having that conversation my angel, I'm so proud of you." She says teasingly giving my sloppy kisses. I squeal squirming around trying to free myself.

"Jasmine, leave my baby alone." Mommy says pulling me away. "And you young lady need a mouth soaping for all the dirt I heard coming out of your mouth a few minutes ago." Mommy tells Hafsa.

"Hey! I was only telling the truth. If you weren't so nosey you wouldn't have heard me!" Hafsa responds sassy. I don't know if she knows but she's sassing the wrong person. Mommy tries to grab her but her fingers slip and Hafsa runs off laughing and I follow after her.

We mannaged to shoo the 'mothers' away so we could have some time alone. The room currently looks like a tornado went past it. We were having a little concert singing to our favourite songs and eating all the junk we could find in the house. I'm not too sure mommy's gonna let that slide but oh well.

We're watching a romance movie, it's sort of Hafsa's guilty pleasure and unfortunately for me I'm stuck watching three part romance movies. "Lani, if I'm a potato just tell me." She says dramatically. "Why can't I find someone who loves me like that." I put my hand over her mouth to keep her quiet.

"It's because you look for unrealistic guys like that is why you can't find them." She rolls her eyes pushing my hand away.

"Like you know anything about guys!" She says scoffing.

"Oh is that how it is? At least I wasn't the one who found out I was actually the side chick."

"Shut up! At least he loved me!" She says.

"Aww you poor baby. I thought the same about my dad growing up." I laugh.

"Ouuu!" She says covering her mouth. "Now that's dark!" She says laughing along. We go back to watching the movie before Aunty Jasmine comes over.

"Time to go." She says in sing-song voice. My heart shatters a bit. Hafsa notices my change of mood and grabs my hand rubbing the back of it with her thumb. "What on earth happened here?" Her mother asks looking at the state of the room.

"Mumma, it's really not that bad." Hafsa says scratching the back of her neck.

"Yes it is!" Mommy says picking up a cushion from the floor. "As long as it gets cleaned up I won't be too upset." She says. I eork really slowly to clean up because I don't want Hafsa to leave yet. "You two really didn't need this much junk. I'm going to have a little one with a sugar rush tonight." Mommy says with a raised eyebrow.

"Mommy!" I say and I notice Hafsa gushing at me using "mommy" instead of her name.

Once we're done cleaning up, mommy and I say our goodbyes seeing them off. When I can no longer see their car I turn around wrapping my arms around Mommy's waist, burying my face in her belly.

"Want them to come back." I say softly

"I know my sweet girl." Mommy says picking me up to go back inside. Mommy lays down on the couch with me cuddled on top of her and she pats my bum rhythmically. I put my fingers in my mouth suckling softly. "Those fingers are icky aren't they pumpkin? We should get your binky to suckle on instead." I shake my head not wanting to hear any of it. "Okay, how about we wash those little hands and make brownies?"

"Yes!" I say excited making mommy chuckle.

"Let's go then." She says. I stand up waiting for her to get up as well. I run to the bathroom to wash my hands and mommy comes in after to wash hers too. I wait for her because mommy's being a slow poke right now. "Mommy let's go!" I whine.

"So impatient!" She says finally following me to the kitchen. Mommy takes out everything we're going to need.

"Mommy I do it, I big girl!" I say pushing her away but she hardly even moves.

"I know you are sweetheart but you have to let mommy help you so we actually end up with brownies." I glare a mommy because she's obviously being a meanie. She quickly gives me a peck on the lips making me smile even though I was trying my bestest not to. Ugh!

Thirty

I closed the container of brownies, taking a big bite once It felt safe enough to do so. Mommy walked in while I'm smiling like an idiot at the brownie. "Nollani! I thought I told you no more, young lady." She scolds. I smile at her, trying my best to look cute. "No more," she say, taking my brownie and eating it.

"Mommy! That was mine!" I stomp, folding my arms over my chest.

"What did I say about stomping your foot at me?" Mommy asks, bending over to be at my level.

"You said no stomping my foot at you!" I respond.

"Hmm," she hums. "I'm glad you remember." She says, patting my bottom as if warning me.

"You're lucky I'm sweet because I would've kicked your butt for eating my brownie," I mumble under my breath.

"Get back to doing your work," she tells me, and I do as she says. Mommy was acting very weird this morning. It was very awkward in the car when she drove me to college. It seemed like she wanted to say something, but she still hasn't said anything. I wanted to ask what the matter was, but I didn't want her to tell me something I didn't want to hear.

"Baby, did you eat any fruit today?" she asks. That question was weird enough because typically Mommy wouldn't ask. If she wanted me to have fruit, she would've forced me to have some, like how she forces me to have water.

"No," I respond still focused on my work. Fruits are just as yucky as veggies, especially apples. The peels are so difficult to swallow. Mommy tried giving me one that was peeled, but it still wasn't nice. It doesn't make any sense because apple juice is so yummy. I'm reading the abstract assigned as this week's reading, but I could still feel Mommy's eyes burning me. I look behind me meeting her gaze. "Mommy! What is it?!" I finally ask. I was feeling very self-conscious at that moment.

I really didn't know if she was asking about me eating fruits because I looked fat and needed more of them or if it was just something else. I saw a slight smile on her face that disappears just as quickly as it appeared. "Come here," she says gently. I hesitated for a second but walked over to her. Mommy swiftly pulls me onto her lap, slipping her hands under my shirt to caress my back. I wanted to stop her because I might slip and I had to finish reading the abstract, but it felt too good.

I lean into Mommy, focusing on her fingers on my back, but then she suddenly stopped, making me whine. "I thought you wanted Mommy to tell you what's on her mind," she says. I nod, lifting my head from her chest. Mommy was giving me serious eye contact, which made me squirm a bit because it meant she was very serious. "You know Mommy cares about you, right?" she starts.

"Yes," I nod.

"Your health is really important to me, and Mommy just wants to make sure you're completely healthy. It's really nothing serious but to me as your mommy it is." I'm still maintaining eye contact because I still had no idea where this is going. "But...when was the last time you went potty? And I'm not talking about what you normally do in your diaper every night." I gasp taken aback. If there was a genie close by, I'd wish to disappear from the surface of the earth.

"Mommy!" I groaned, hiding my face in her boobies. Mommy chuckles, rubbing my back as comfort.

"I'm not forcing you to tell me love, but you should be using the potty at least three times a week. Which...I haven't seen you doing," Mommy says.

"No way that's too much." I tell her. Three times a week sounds ridiculous to me.

"Yes way! Mommy thinks you've been having way too much bread for lunch and not enough breastmilk to help you pass it out," she responds. "Suppositories would do the trick, but I'd rather we try milk first." What the hell are suppositories?

"Milk? Like now?! But I'm big," I say, looking at her boobies.

"That's not what your eyes are telling me," she said, booping my nose, reminding me to blink. I was waiting for her to undo the buttons on her shirt. Like, is she going to give me my milk already or no? She finally unbuttons her shirt, taking it off before pulling down her bra to expose both her breasts. My cheeks could fry an egg right now. She guides my head to her nipple, and I suckle contently once I was latched on.

The aim was to stay big today so I could do my work, but obviously, Mommy had other plans. I closed my eyes, feeling my milky start to fill my belly. I played with Mommy's hair because it was the only thing that looked interesting right now, that's until I noticed her exposed boobie. I reached over to grab it, but Mommy props me up and guides me to latch onto it. I suckle until I start barely getting any more milk.

"Mommy, all done?" I ask, trying to squeeze some more milk out, but there was none.

"Yes sweetie, it's all in your belly now," she says poking my belly, making me giggle. "What's so funny?" she asks, poking my belly again and making me giggle more. "Oh! Mommy found the giggle button." she says, poking every inch of my belly. I became a ball of giggles until I accidentally tooted. Mommy laughs at my little accident.

"Not funny! Mommy's fault," I pout.

"There's no need to be embarrassed my love. It's going to be a secret just between the two of us...unless your stuffies heard it too," she teased.

"Mommy no, they not hear it!" I tried to defend myself, feeling embarrassed. It wasn't so loud that my stuffies could hear it all the way upstairs ...Right? I got off Mommy's lap, upset with her, and bury my face on the arm of the couch, not wanting to talk to her anymore.

"Aww, come now, Mommy was just teasing," she says pulling me back onto her lap. "So sensitive!" she says, kissing me. I'm still upset, not really moved by her kisses. "Fine, what can Mommy do to earn your trust?" She asks, she's definitely going to regret it.

"B-ownie!" I shout, grinning from ear to ear.

"Oh but that belly's still so full!" she says, looking at my belly.

"Nuh-uh, have space for b'ownie. See!" I show her there's still space by popping my belly in and out. Mommy chuckles fixing her bra. She stands up with me in her arms to get me my brownie. I knew I had her wrapped around my finger.

"I'll let you have one more. Just because you're so sweet and didn't 'kick my butt'." she says air quoting. I squeak hiding my face in her chest, realising she heard me mumbling earlier. I can never win against her at this point.

Thirty One

Hanaina's POV

Nollani's having a bit of a tough morning. At first, she didn't want me to hold her, but once I got her in my arms, she wouldn't let me put her down. She isn't really talking, just nodding and shaking her head. I'm not sure what's going on in her head.

"Can you tell Mommy what's wrong, baby?" I ask, and she points to her chest. "Your chest hurts?" I ask, rubbing my hand over her chest, hoping to make it a little better. I'm wondering if she's feeling sick again, but she looks perfectly healthy. She pushes my hand away and points at her chest again, seeming frustrated. "Can you use your words, please?" I say, a bit firmly because I'm also starting to get frustrated.

"Heart hurts," she says so adorably, making some of my frustration fade.

"Why is it sore, bubs? What happened?" I ask, running my nails on her back. I see her eyes well up with tears, and she's avoiding eye contact.

"You no love me, you leaving me," she sniffles, laying her head on my chest. I have no idea where this is coming from. I don't remember saying anything that could possibly make her feel like I don't love her. In fact, I told her just how much I loved her before she fell asleep last night. She was in a good mood, so this isn't making any sense. It could've been a bad dream, that's my best guess.

"It's okay, baby, no need to cry. Was it a bad dream?" She nods, confirming my suspicions. Her little body's shaking like a leaf. I hold her tightly against my chest, whispering words of comfort. I lift her chin up, wiping away the tears on her face. "Do you know why you had that dream?" I ask gently. She shakes her head, her eyes full of curiosity. "Mommy thinks you're subconsciously constantly worried about me leaving you, and that's why you had that dream. I'm not going anywhere used" I tell her, planting a kiss on her forehead.

"Mommy not leaving me?" she asks, which hurts me because I can only imagine how many people have abandoned her when she needed them the most. Her grandmother and Hafsa are the only ones who have really stuck around for her. I know her mother's absence has really triggered her because she thrives around maternal figures. I'm doing my best to be the mommy she needs.

"Pumpkin, I'm not leaving you. Mommy loves you too much. I love you just as much when you're being a cheeky little girl." I say, tapping her nose. She looks up at me as if taking in every little detail on my face. I smile at her, rubbing my thumb against her cheek. She returns the smile, but it's accompanied by a glint of mischief in her eyes. "Lani!" I warn gently, receiving giggles.

"Mommyyyy!" she whines, pouting cutely at me.

"Tell me what it is, then I'll give you a fitting response." She smiles, giving me a kiss on the cheek just to butter me up. I just know she's about to ask for my whole arm.

"No school today," she says.

"No!" I get up, throwing her over my shoulder.

"I help Mommy at work," she says, kicking her feet.

"You've had enough work trips with me," I tell her, setting her on my hip.

"One more. I be a good girl," she says, giving me puppy eyes.

"Let's get you a bath, then I'll decide after."

"Otay."

"That's a good girl," I praise. I leave the room, going into the bathroom, filling the tub with water, and letting her add the toys she wants to play with. I'm struggling with a very independent little one who wants to take off her own clothes but can't get her nightie over her head. I sigh, pulling the nightie off and finally her diaper.

I set her in the tub. One minute I have everything under control and the next she splashes me and my shirt and pants are soaked. I'm about to give her an ear full but her little laugh softens me up. I shake my head accepting defeat. I notice her staring at my breasts but I shake it off. We decided that she isn't allowed breastmilk in the mornings because she gets milk drunk and gives me a tough time getting her ready.

"That's enough splashing for now little fish." I pull her out of the bathtub, wiping her dry. "Go get dressed, your clothes are on your bed." I say deciding to go dry my clothes in the meantime because I'm not picking another outfit. Nollani is singing at the top of her lungs which is a normal occurrence when she's in a good mood. I dry my clothes using the hairdryer and once I switch it off, I realise how quiet it is.

I quickly walk to her room and find her clothes untouched. Her froggy towel is thrown on the floor. I go into her playroom and she standing completely naked in front of her doll house. "Nollani!" I call her, and she's startled. I adjust my glasses over the bridge of my nose, peering at her above them. Experience has taught me I tend to intimidate people a lot more when I do that. "I asked you to get dressed. You didn't even bother to wear your underwear." She pouts not saying anything. "Come," I call her holding out my hand for her to hold.

"Two seconds mommy, I coming." She tries to negotiate. I lift my eyebrows and that does the job. "Not fair!" She whines folding her arms leaving me hanging. I follow her into her room, grabbing a pull up from the drawer. I walk over to sit on the bed to get her dressed. "No! want panties mommy!" She yells stomping her foot. I pull her in between my legs giving her bottom two swats.

"You don't stomp your foot at me, I gave you enough warnings!" I say looking in her eyes, noticing they're slightly glossy. I get her dressed quickly and sit her on my lap. I'm about to address the stomping issue but she doesn't let me say a word.

"Sowwy mommy, no more stomping. P'omise." She says leaning her forehead against mine.

"It's all good, lovebug. Thank you for apologising." I kiss her forehead. "I love you." I tell her.

"I love you too." She says melting my heart. "You decide now?" She asks. I'm puzzled for a second before I figure out what she's on about.

"Yes sweetie you can come with Mommy, only because you're so adorable and Mommy can't tell you no." I mumbled the last part. There's suddenly a loud screech. I hold the bridge on my nose realising it's going to be a long day. I do her hair quickly because we're already running late. I pack her breakfast so she can have it in the car to save time. I make myself coffee because I really deserve it this morning.

When we get to the office, Nollani doesn't even waste time, leaving for Latisha's office. A few minutes later my door swings open and I'm met with an angry Latisha, Nollani comes running after. I raise my eyebrows waiting for Latisha to say something. She folds her arms over her chest but I noticed her hands trembling.

"You didn't have to smack her, so what if she stomps her foot?!" Latisha says stomping her foot, testing me. I close the file I was looking at, standing up from my chair. I walk over to the two girls standing in front of me, towering over the both of them. Latisha places her hands behind her, I know she's protecting her bottom because she used to do the same thing while she was my little. Nollani shuffles slowly, hiding behind Latisha. I'm very amused by this little confrontation.

I place my finger under her chin, "Stomp your foot again and I'll show you 'so what'."

www.ingramcontent.com/pod-product-compliance
Lightning Source LLC
Chambersburg PA
CBHW072210070526
44585CB00015B/1270

www.ingramcontent.com/pod-product-compliance
Lightning Source LLC
Chambersburg PA
CBHW072211070526
44585CB00015B/1291